THE RALLYI

THE RALLYING POINT

BY

MELVIN CHARLES

BRYANT AND DILLON PUBLISHERS,INC.
ORANGE, NEW JERSEY

Copyright © 1994 by Melvin Charles

Edited by Hazel Lockett

Photographs courtesy of Melvin Charles

Library of Congress Cataloging in Publication Data
Charles, Melvin
1.The Rallying Point 2. History   3. Black American Heritage Flag
(A BRYANT and DILLON Book)
CIP# 93-74944
ISBN 0-9638672-1-0

Printed in The United States of America
10 9 8 7 6 5 4 3 2 1

To the memory of
Gleason T. Jackson.

Prologue

The street was crowded. The noises of the rush hour traffic might have crept into our consciousness any other day but this one. The blustery cold air was right for that March day. Blistering currents of wind brushed the city's debris past us. I leaned back in the cold air, tilting my head upward. My eyes, crossing the grey facade of Newark's City Hall, caught sight of a wind-whipped American flag.

There it was! Folding and flapping, stretching out its length and turning again on itself in the March wind -- another flag. Flying at the top of a silver pole, alongside the Stars and Stripes, in front of City Hall in Newark, New Jersey, United States of America, the Black American Flag.

I turned to look at Gleason. He stood with his slight frame poised against the wind, hands in overcoat pockets, a gently radiant smile on his face.

We shook hands once, again, and grinned proudly at each other. We had done it. Our obsession was a reality. Our flag was flying.

A policeman neared, telling us to move from the No Parking spot. As we came down the steps a young black girl passed. I couldn't resist. I pointed to the flag and asked her whether she knew what it was.

She answered, "That's the flag for black people." She kept on walking.

We rode home in silence. Wrapped in our pride and joy and moments too big for words on that fifth day of March, 1968.

Gleason drove. I thought back to the beginning of this reality we had created and lived with for almost a year.

Chapter 1

I headed out to the neighborhood bakery early for bread and milk. Gleason had called the night before and asked me to stop by after church. His invitations were common place, and his voice gave no indication of urgency.

Gleason a was a good friend. Like me, he was young, married. Both of us had a young daughter, our wives worked, we pulled our share at our jobs. Gleason was foreman at a chemical plant, and I worked as a display designer for a freelance outfit. We were active in the Jaycees and the Fourth Ward Political Club in Linden, New Jersey. He was an ardent churchgoer; I was a backslider--too many years of being the "deacon's son."

Often he and I talked late into the night about our time,the mid-1960s. The excitement of the civil rights movement was beginning to change in texture and direction we thought. We also thought our intense discussions would reveal this new texture and direction. Our guts still churned at the thought of bombs taking out four little girls in a Birmingham church and of dogs, electric prods, and water hoses knocking out blacks in the south. We sensed that street marches and demonstrations were too charged with the potential for death to last much longer and that blacks would not wait for peaceful, non-violent acts to solve our problems. But where was the "movement" going? What new direction would our leaders chart?

Our discussions yielded no answers. We did discover that we stood on the same ground, expecting something positive and good would come out of the turmoil. The fever would break after four hundred years and a race of people would be able to walk forth whole, well, feeling good about themselves. We held these positive thoughts though we were not marchers, had never been to jail for the cause or for any other reason. He and I were part of that great mass of blacks who wanted our rights, peace, brotherhood, and equality. We had talked often of our need to see a feeling of pride emerge among our neighbors, our black brothers and sisters. There was much to be proud of in our heritage; we were survivors as a people. We didn't think we heard that often enough. The rhetoric of our leaders often urged people to the streets in anger and not often enough in pride.

It was pride in the heritage of Black people that started us on a cause that would absorb us completely. Thinking back on it now, it is incredible that one simple question began the "crusade."

I drove to Gleason's house that Sunday. He met me at the door and we climbed the steps to his apartment on the second floor of his two-family home. His daughter April met me at the top of the steps and asked how I was feeling. Gleason was finishing dinner and offered me dessert. I declined but took a cup of tea and sat and waited to hear what was on his mind. Later we sat in his living room and spent a few minutes talking about the sermon he had heard at church that morning. He toyed with his unlit pipe as he talked. Then his voice grew softer and the little tremor it sometimes had seemed to lay back as the words came out strong and hung in the middle of that Sunday afternoon. There was an idea he had been thinking about for a couple of months and he wanted to bounce it off me. Quietly he asked, "I wonder how it would be if black people had a flag?"

I absorbed his words and thought on them for a long moment. The question was unexpected, a sudden shock. Just as quietly, I finally asked whether there had ever been a flag for Black Americans, or as we were known then, Negroes. We thought back over childhood experiences in NAACP and Urban League youth groups, saw again the inside of our churches and schools. Nowhere did our recollections surface a flag. Later I would remember having heard Malcolm X say that black people seemed to feel they had so little to be proud of and nothing to represent them, that black people didn't even have a flag to carry in a parade. That recollection didn't emerge that Sunday afternoon. We just knew that there was no flag for black people.

We talked for a long time that day, sometimes past each other, weaving together with our words the threads of our shared thinking. We ranged over the words and the works of Paul Robeson, Martin Luther King and Adam Clayton Powell, wondering what they would have thought about the flag. We talked about the local leadership in our city and the quiet way Blacks reacted to the snowballing discontent among the country's black population. Our conversation jumped and tumbled, returning every few minutes to ask one, then another question. What should a flag look like? What colors should it have? How could we go about putting it together?

We talked for four hours or more. The words poured out of me as the idea generated question after question. Gleason reacted and responded in his quiet, reserved way, braking the speed of my questions with his long-held certainty that a flag would be right for the times and the people who would rally to it. We wound up in a lingering silence. A bond of awe wrapped around us at the audacity of the idea---a flag for black Americans. We'd have to sit down again, soon, to talk about it more. There was nothing else that could be said that night.

When I got home my wife wanted to know what the big discussion had been about. I told her simply that Gleason had suggested that we design a flag that would represent black people. She said aloud the same words that had echoed in my head on the drive home, "A flag?" We stood there looking at each other as her question floated in the air. It was easy to see her mind ranging over the same questions he and I had asked each other. She didn't say anything else, and I couldn't have responded if she had. I needed time to think about the idea and wanted to be alone to do it.

I went upstairs seeking solitude, little realizing that my daughter, Joy, was right behind me almost walking on my heels. She wanted to play in our usual evening ritual just before her bed time. We spent a few minutes together but didn't get too deeply into the story-telling games we both enjoyed. I gave her a kiss, urged her off to bed, then fell into my bed and closed my eyes and thought about the flag.

A flag! Why not?

Why not indeed!

We talked again the next day. We never asked ourselves why, why should there be a flag for black people? That question was buried under the more serious questions that nagged at us. Why had there never been a flag that black people responded to, wore in miniature on their lapels, pasted on the bumpers of their cars, carried in a parade like the Irish, or the Italians, or the Polish, or any other ethnic group? Why weren't there commemorative holidays on which a flag could be out front? What was it that black people didn't have that existed among other ethnic groups in this country? THEY all marched proudly with the American flag on one side and the flag of their heritage on the other. We black people walked with the American flag and the Masonic emblem or the lodge, or church banner, but never with something that said anything about our heritage. We, too, had a past, a heritage lost in the years of separation from our roots, a heritage rich in its diversity of tribes and languages and customs, but a heritage stemming from Mother Africa that was common to all of us. Why had it never been that we had a flag to represent that heritage, that oneness overriding diversity?

We searched for answers to those questions. We spent hours trying to figure out why this had not been a reality before. Then it dawned on us that if we kept talking about why it had never been, we would never get to the business of making it happen. The conversation turned then. We began to talk about what the flag should be like.

It sounds simple to say - "Design a flag." With a whole spectrum of colors from which to choose, simplicity went out the window even when it was easy to settle on the first color. It had to be black. With that first decision about the flag, we came to a dead stop. Neither of us could say what should come next. This wasn't going to be easy. The choice of colors was critical; the colors would have to represent something important to black people and neither of us wanted a snap decision, hastily made and meaningless. The flag would have to make a point and do it effectively, cleanly, and appeal to the eye and the heart. We would have to go about this slowly, deliberately, carefully.

A few days later, Gleason and I and our wives attended the Fourth Ward Political Club breakfast, an annual affair. On the drive over, we talked about the possibility of approaching the National Director of CORE who was to be guest speaker. We wanted to see how the idea of a flag might sound to someone of his stature. We had talked independently with our wives about the idea and they had given encouragement and support. Neither recognized the immensity of the task we were setting for ourselves. Neither did we.

We never got to speak with James Farmer that day. We listened to him talk of a need for black people to have power, to establish and use power in their communities, and to show pride in themselves. Gleason and I smiled at each other as Farmer's words poured out. He was aiming at some of the very things we had talked about in the last few evenings. I traced an invisible rectangle on the white tablecloth in front of me as Farmer talked and thought to myself, "This is a flag and in the middle of it we're going to put something that will bring pride to the hearts of all Negroes". How ambitious! Gleason caught my eye as the outline of the unseen flag was traced. He probably thought, as I did listening still to Farmer, that we were going to make our contribution to showing pride in ourselves.

Farmer's speech was received enthusiastically by the audience. He was surrounded by the crowd at the end of the program and since we were just ticket-buyers and not organizers of the breakfast we had no entree to him for any length of time. It was just as well though. We felt good about what he had said and what we were about to do. His words cemented our resolve to plunge totally into the business of creating this flag.

The following Wednesday evening we sat at the table in my basement. Around us on the walls were posters of Dick Gregory in one of his typical poses, a black Santa Claus, Bill Cosby. They looked down at us as we tried to develop a set of colors that would be appropriate to represent black people. We chose red as the second base color. Red was for the blood that black people had shed for human justice and human dignity and in defense of this country since its beginning.

Black and red. Agreed, but not enough.

Another color was needed, we thought. We looked at paint chips and color swatches brought home from the display house. Blues, browns, greens, oranges, all the permutations of these colors. Finally, we chose gold. Gold for prosperity and everlasting life. Who could not relate to gold?

It was decided. This flag would be black, red, and gold!

How would these colors be placed in relationship to each other? It took hours to cut and juggle strips of paper. We cut stripes, stars, rectangles, bars, moving them around, eyeing arrangements. Bands and stripes lay atop each other until the last field of black emerged as the diagonal center of the flag. Two acute triangles of red, one at the upper right of the black field, one at the lower left, completed it. It was not a mimic of the stars and stripes. It was a vastly different arrangement of colors and one we found pleasing to the eye.

Still it was incomplete. The gold had to be shaped into a design on the black field. We talked about a number of things that might be put there as a representation of some event or concept important to Negroes. Maybe a globe would represent the places we had traveled over the world, caught in the black diaspora our ancestors had experienced. Maybe a cotton mill or a bale would be appropriate to memorialize the burden our people had carried so unwillingly on their backs as slaves. It would be a reminder of the ugly and bitter immensity of atrocities wreaked on our forebears. But then, we agreed, who needs reminders of the past? We could see the residue of slavery in the living conditions of black people in the 1960's, the poverty and unemployment and hunger of millions, the sense of being burdened still by the acts of the past. It was an easy jump then to talk about the symbolism of a sword on the flag. It would represent the anger and frustration of a people deprived of so much in the land of plenty. When we reached that point in our discussion, it was plain that we were not thinking in a positive vein. Anger and frustration were not what we wanted to express in this flag. We wanted it to tell of hope and not hatred, plenty and not poverty, peace and not turmoil.

It was not easy to focus on thinking positively when we were surrounded with all the oppression of black people in America that characterized the 1960's. It was not easy that night to choose a symbol that could speak fairly of positive thoughts black people might hold. We sat back and looked at the red and black diagonals and then at the gold paper that would evolve somehow into a symbol with real meaning.

Before the evening ended, we fell into a fast moving discussion of what we might do with a flag once it was completely designed. We sometimes talked at the same time, sometimes found ourselves in silence when we reached no agreement and knew that somehow we would have to keep ideas flowing. At one point the question of whether to get a patent for the flag arose. Would we run the risk of having someone take the idea and the design and prostitute it for money if we had no patent? Or, was it a copyright we needed? In our naivete we didn't know. We just agreed that we would have to find out how to protect the flag.

We talked, too, about who we could get to work with us to take the flag to the people. Our discussion focused on the city and the people in it, each of us repeating refrains from conversations we had had long before the flag was ever an idea brewing in Gleason's head. Linden seemed occupied mostly by honorable, peaceful people who stayed to themselves and did what the status quo said one must do. Our conversations with neighbors and acquaintances in the community had not turned up too many kindred spirits. There was a feeling of near apathy, certainly not any real measure of aggressiveness, among those to whom we talked in the aftermath of civil rights crises of recent times. Probably the average high school student was more cognizant of those crises and more prone to voice his desire to do something about the status of black people than his parents were. We would have to defer the search for people to help in the task of letting the world know about the flag. It wasn't even on the drawing board yet.

We must have sat for three or four hours, ranging again and again over the colors and symbols, the things we needed to do to transform this idea into reality and then to have others see, understand, and accept it. Somehow, we felt, everything would work out. It had to. Creating this flag was going to be our contribution to the struggle that many black people had not fully sensed. That struggle, we thought, was to find and exhibit pride in ourselves as a race of people.

It grew late. Gleason was exhilarated though we had made no major step forward in finishing the design or in settling the many questions raised as we talked. He held his pipe in his mouth for a few minutes as he stood at the door and then said, in his usual gentle, reflective manner, "We may be making history, maybe not. It's a challenge. I'm glad we're working on it together. I think we can do it."

"Doing it" soon meant hours of research. It had seemed such a simple thing to select some colors, draw a symbol, have it made up, go out into the world and announce it. It just didn't work that way.

I came to know the libraries in Elizabeth and Newark well. The librarians got to know me, too, as I sought their help in finding the books that were needed. I must have pored over every volume on flags and all the black history books in the Newark library. Reading black history books took little time. There were only a few there to read. Each evening after work, I headed straight to a library until satisfied that there were no records of a flag designed specifically for or by black Americans.

Volume after volume passed through my hands as I examined pictures of flags representing some phase of American history or the American people. One author described the American flag as "... the very poetry of motion." Another said that the flag represented a people seeking redress of grievances and finding it, ultimately, in independence. I learned of the relationship between the stars of the flag and the Navy of the colonies, that a naval flagmaker had replaced the original heraldic six pointed star with a five pointed "molet" just so that star would not blur into a messy dot across several leagues of ocean. Visibility was essential. The symbol of this flag had to be seen clearly so its meaning would not be lost.

I discovered that the United States of America did not have an "official" flag until 1912. This nation had existed for nearly one hundred and twenty-five years without having confirmed by law the arrangement of stars and the relative proportions of parts of the banner. An executive order issued by William Howard Taft in June of 1912 standardized the American flag just in time to hoist it in the battlefields of World War I. All the etiquette associated with the flag came into being with the Flag Code in 1942. That was after Gleason and I were born. The American flag seemed to be as officially new as it could be. If it took from 1777 to 1912 to get a national flag put firmly into place, we would have to take our vitamins and prepare to stay around for awhile with this one we were dreaming about!

It was amazing to learn of the number and variety of flags that have been carried by people representing some viewpoint, some group, some part of American history. There had been the flags of Old Congress Hall and many regiments and battalions in the Continental Army. There had been a Rattlesnake flag, the Pine Tree flag, the Green Mountain Boys had one of their own, the Alamo had flown a special banner. Washington's Life Guards, the South Carolina Navy, the Society of Cincinnati, and Fort Sumter had each flown separate flags. There was once the Confederate Stars and Bars, the Confederate Southern Cross and the Confederate White Man's Flag.

The word "unfurl" came to life as flag etiquette jumped out at me from the pages of the books taken to the corner tables in the Newark Library and read until closing time each night.

I took to that corner all the atlases, history books, anything that might give a hint of how nations and peoples had represented themselves with a banner. Flags of the African nations drew my attention particularly as I tried in vain to find a common denominator of colors, patterns, symbols, designs.

One day, wearying of the hours in the libraries, I drove over to the United Nations building just to stand and look at the flags. The array of banners was mind-boggling. So many, so different from each other. One flag might share the same colors with its neighbors yet be totally unlike in arrangement of those colors. It was plain that each nation, each people, had somehow chosen one flag to speak for them, to say to the rest of the world, "This is our flag, our rallying point."

I wondered, as I stood in the UN Plaza, who had created those flags and how many people and how much time had been needed for consensus before the flags gained recognition and meaning and acceptance. There were no answers to my unspoken questions. There was only the compelling need to leave that plaza and get on to the business of putting together this flag that could tell of pride in heritage and history.

I read books on African history intently. The majesty of the ancient kingdoms of Ghana, Mali, and Songhay leaped from the pages. Descriptions of bronze and terra cotta sculptures aroused great interest. It was exciting to learn of the antiquity of the sculptures and of rock murals picturing pastoral civilizations dating back to more than 5000 B.C. As I read I came to understand the spirit weaving through black people and surfacing in those early works of art. Those pastoral civilizations had loved the rich African soil, found that its fruits sustained peoples without avaricious adoration of the gold and diamonds and metals buried beneath the surface.

I was impressed with the history of Ethiopia and its relationship with its contemporaries -- Egypt, Nubia, Assyria and Phoenicia. The value and worth of the African nations and soil were evident in the constant assaults on the continent made by Greek intellectuals, Roman adventurers, European and American explorers, missionaries, empire builders and exploiters. Africa's greatest treasure -- its people -- had been systematically raped as the great slave machines of the empires swept across its face. Africa and its people must have been of value, otherwise why bother to rape the continent? Who takes a thing that has no value? And, who but the mindless believe that you can put a price, a slave price, on the human race?

How had black people responded to the diaspora? Had they ever reunified themselves with any symbol of the heritage that had been ripped away from them -- their languages, customs, arts, cultures? I could find no symbol of that unity, that remembrance of past, or emerging sense of present pride in self. I did read about Marcus Garvey and the Black Star flag he had flown over his ship in the Back-to-Africa Movement of the early twenties. That was not what we wanted to symbolize. We were not trying to portray a movement of revolution or a back-to-Africa groundswell.

We felt that a symbol of pride was needed badly by oppressed people, a people who had very little hand in any major business, made no decisions in this country. In a way, maybe, the biggest thing black people had going for them in 1967 was the statue of Abraham Lincoln in Washington, D.C. We could always stand on the steps at his feet and feel that we had safety, a haven, a marble soapbox from which to speak of our dreams, our hopes, our needs.

Certainly black heroes were few and far between. The mainstream of black people had heard of a George Washington Carver and a Marion Anderson. Their names were in the used history books that arrived in many classrooms for black children after having been ravaged in the schools across the tracks. The richness of the Harlem Renaissance and the emerging revisionist writings of serious black historians had not yet reached into the schools where our black children were being taught. Black people seemed to have so little access to the testimony of history that they had worth, yet, that worth was woven into the fabric, cotton and otherwise, of the totality of American life.

We seemed to stand naked as a people without the sure knowledge of a rich past to give us warmth. Gleason and I wanted to synthesize what we knew of that past and to meld it with the hopes we continued to have for the future and have it all come together in a flag, the symbol of a people.

This sense of making a contribution grew stronger each day as my research made it clearer that there was no single unifying symbol with which black people could identify. We wanted to create such a symbol yet we found the task of choosing the elements of that symbol to be incredible in magnitude. How was one to find a simple yet powerful image to place on the field of black and red we had chosen? What could have meaning to the generation caught in the daily bombardment of marches, water hosings, jailings and painful reminders of second class citizenship?

Finally, we did not seek to portray the struggle of the '60's. It became indefinitely more important to find pride in what had been an unheralded but glorious past in our African heritage. It was essential to convey somehow the strength that lay in a people who had survived the wretchedness of slavery. It was important, even more, to give the world a glimpse of what we as a people wanted to characterize as our future. Our black leaders had already said it, but the message wasn't heard too clearly as the rhetoric rolled from stages and platforms. Black people wanted peace and prosperity. Surcease from barely buried memories of slave crossings, "breaking-in" plantations, lost families, rootlessness.

We labored, Gleason and I, to distill the waters of our people's history as we had come to know it. We wanted to create a symbol that reflected the rising sense of strength among black people yet tempered with a sign of the desire for peace.

We decided to put a sword on the flag, after all. A sword would surely represent strength, authority, power. What that sword should look like was another matter.

By chance I came across a picture of an Eighth-century Moorish boarding sword on one of my library visits. I had gone through stacks of books on swords hoping to find one or two drawings that would trigger the good gut reaction we wanted. It appeared suddenly in front of me. No sword is made that way by accident. When it is deliberately blunted, a more powerful authority emerges. In a way, it is an abdication of the power to kill.

We chose that blunted sword for the flag without hesitation. Later our parents reminded us of Isaiah 2:4.

> He shall judge between the nations
> And shall decide for many people:
> And they shall beat their swords into
> Plowshares, and their spears into
> Pruning hooks; Nations shall not lift
> Up sword against nation, neither shall
> They learn war any more.

Even with this symbol now firmly fixed in the center of the field of black, we felt the design was still unfinished. Something was needed to soften the harsher implications of even a blunted sword. One evening as we talked again about symbols and meanings, I idly drew a wreath of fig leaves around the sword on the sketch pad that was always the focal point on the table between us. In my Navy days I had seen the women of the Middle East and East African coasts walking proudly with baskets of figs on their heads. Figs were presented by custom to visitors to a home in that part of the world and seemed to represent an offer to the visitor to take of the earth's bounty. This ancient and beautiful life-giving fruit held special meaning to the peoples of the African continent; when one had figs one did not want. It seemed right to symbolize the prosperity we sought as a people with a wreath of fig leaves. This would be a link to the past and a hope for the future.

Suddenly the design was complete!

It had taken several weeks to get all the elements of the flag together, but now it was all there--black, red, gold, a blunted sword, a wreath of fig leaves. These would embody the pride we wanted the flag to stimulate and represent!

Making the design flag in full size was the next step. The small free-lance outfit where I worked was located only a quarter-mile from my house. It was easy to go back to the shop in the evenings and use my workbench as the delivery table for the design flag. The shop was a good place to be to let creative juices flow; it was filled with props--moons, starbursts, suns, papiermache heads of animals, cut out letters, flowers hanging in bunches and loops. It was an instant wonderland; a child could stay there for days in total joy letting his imagination run into every fantasy from Santa's workshop to outer space. For me, though, it was filled with the materials that were needed to turn creative thoughts into reality. The pressure of my work lay in knowing that there was the opportunity to persuade people to buy through the work of my hands. It was a good place, too, because I was still learning the craft and there were good people in the shop who taught me freely the nuances of design and display.

For three evenings, Gleason and I worked there after hours making the design flag. Each night we would take home whatever had been completed leaving no traces that we had been there.

We worked with large sheets of cardboard for the backing. Hours went into selecting the right shade of red, painting in the diagonal stripes of black and red, and carefully laying on the gold glitter for the blunted sword and fig leaf wreath. We made two models, each 2 1/2' X 4' large. When the first was finished, we looked at it for a long time, savoring the pleasure of the moment. It was exactly what we wanted. In one more evening we finished the second design flag and took that one to my house. (The first had gone to Gleason's home.) When we had hung it in my basement, we sat for hours asorbing the look of it, the colors, the design, feeling such quiet joy in the act of having created it.

The next step would be to make one of fabric, we decided. And, we thought, the colonies had had Betsy Ross to make the flag for them so why shouldn't we get two patient wives to make this flag of fabric for us?

We wanted a natural fiber for the material and I made it my business while moving among supply houses during the day to pick up extra pieces of black cotton, a couple of yards of red, some gold. It took a few days to accumulate enough for our needs as I asked casually here and there for a few odds and ends of fabric. Nobody minded and nobody asked why it was needed. When we had enough, we laid it in neat bundles before our wives and asked their assistance. They agreed enthusiastically and we spent an exciting afternoon planning ways to make a real family package out of the flag- making day. The sewing machine was at my house and it was natural to make that the work place. Gleason's wife would do the sewing; my wife would put the dinner together. Our daughters could play together while I would do the layout and cutouts. Gleason's responsibility was to supervise the children and coordinate everybody's activities.

We started about one o'clock in the afternoon on Sunday, April 26th. The work begun to flow as soon as we gathered; the girls scampered off to play in Joy's room, pots and pans started to move in the kitchen, the sewing machine was oiled and threaded. I laid out the fabric on a table in the basement and began cutting the black and red diagonals. It was real tedious and exacting work trying to make sure the bias sections would come together as we wanted. As soon as the first two pieces were cut, Gleason and I went upstairs to watch as they were stitched together. From that point on, it was constant movement between the basement and the TV room where the sewing was going on, into the kitchen to check on progress with dinner, upstairs to look in on the girls. Often during the afternoon the layout didn't work and we had to start again, especially with the fig leaf wreath. Everybody got a little cranky and edgy. It was total chaos when the fabric slipped off the sewing machine and my hands grabbed at it, trying to keep everything in place. We got in each other's way more often than not.

Suddenly, about five thirty that evening, it was done. Gleason's wife, Mariam, sat back from the sewing machine. My wife, sensing the quite in the room, left the kitchen and joined us as we stood by the machine. Joy and April appeared without being called.

We looked at it. The cotton glistened, the golden wreath and sword shone against the vivid black and red diagonals. We held it out between the four of us, the girls peeking above the edges to see what absorbed us. After a while, Gleason took the flag from us and held it against his chest, holding his arms around it, not speaking. The cloth was warm as he handed it to me after a long moment. It was passed among us until the younger child held it quietly, looking at us with eyes wide open as she wrapped her tiny arms around it. Nobody said anything; the moment was solemn and intense. The flag we had made that day captured the essence of our thoughts, our intentions, our desires. Somehow, we were sure , all black people would feel as we did that day--proud, proud of this flag, proud of ourselves and what we had accomplished in those few hours.

Chapter 2

In only a little more than a month we had moved from idea to reality. The design flag lay now on the table in the recreation room, there to be examined and analyzed again for its content. We left it there; that seemed the only thing to do with it. For the next week or two Gleason and I talked several times a day trying to decide what might be the reasonable next step to take. In the evenings we would sit in my basement and look at the cardboard design on the wall and the design flag on the table and ponder again whether to seek help from others to begin to spread the news of the flag. We surveyed the community mentally once again and, as before, failed to think readily of anyone who would grasp the significance and magnitude of what we felt we were about to do. Yet, we could not define for ourselves what it was we had to do or could do with the help of others from the community. We had no game plan, no great strategy to use to let the world know of the existence of the flag. At last we took the easiest route we could think of to make the "birth announcement" to the world.

I took pictures of the cardboard design while Gleason hauled out an old typewriter. Night after night we beat out what we called letters of introduction and sent them, one hundred of them, to black men and women who could understand and appreciate what the flag was about. It had been easy to decide on those people; they had all been listed and pictured in *Ebony* magazine in the annual feature - "100 Most Influential Negroes".

We took a post-office box in nearby Roselle and each day we mailed the letters, secure in our sense that a responsive chord would sound in one hundred bells within a matter of days. One of us checked the post office daily and made the call to the other to give the report. Empty. The box stayed empty. There were no 100-bell salutes for our effort. Not one of the "one hundred most influential Negroes" responded.

While we waited in great anticipation for the deluge of mail, we kept moving and doing. We had decided to go for a patent.

We called around to friends who had gotten patents and asked where and how you go about doing it. Friends wanted to know "what"? We didn't tell them. Finally, somebody gave us the name of a patent attorney in New York City and we made an appointment for May 16th.

The attorney's office was not too impressive but he had enough diplomas and certificates and affiliation letters hanging on the walls in the small comfortable office. We looked at them and felt we were in good hands. He was in his early forties, vital, articulate. He seemed very interested in what we presented once we began to talk about it and when we held up the design flag we had brought with us, he leaned back in his chair, put his hands behind his head and looked at it for a long time. It was impossible to know what he was thinking; his lawyer face gave away no inkling of what was in his head. It was agony waiting for him to say something and when he offered the thought, in a musing sort of way, that nobody had ever done THAT before, my heart skipped a beat.

He said it as though he had flipped over all the index cards in his brain and found none that showed a flag for black people. What we had in our hands just had to be original!

It was easy to talk about fees and to listen to the man tell us what was involved in a patent search. We heard him say that if there were another flag with a design or colors in any similar we would have to change ours to preserve originality. We understood that, but felt that we would not have to make any changes and that when the progress report on the patent search arrived in three weeks it would corroborate the uniqueness of the flag.

The days passed slowly during those three weeks. We checked the post office for the daily dose of no news. Each day we expected there would be that first letter signalling interest and recognition from the influential black brothers and sisters and each day there was disappointment. The attorney came through right on schedule, though. Three weeks to the day he called to say he had received information from Washington. A search in the Patent Office Archives showed that there was no flag representing Negro Americans. The only symbolic representation registered there was a drawing of a purple and yellow flag with an image of a Negro man in a high top hat, pants too short, tight spats on his feet striding along with a chicken in one hand and a watermelon under the other arm!

The attorney gave us a copy of the patent search letter and told us "full speed ahead". Four weeks later the patent pending notification arrived. When we held that piece of paper in our hands, we knew we were beginning the journey to the world outside our two homes.

The design flag still lay on the table. No one outside immediate families had seen it until one evening a young cousin of mine stopped by with her mother for a short visit before she was to leave for college. I invited them down to the basement without telling them what they would see. In a way, I wanted to see what their first reactions would be to the flag without giving any context to it. They stood there and murmured that they thought it was "nice," "colorful," "an interesting design". When I told them what it was the atmosphere changed. The mother put her hands on her hips and smiled broadly! My cousin grinned and said, "Hey, that's all right!"

Before they left that evening I heard from them the words that would be repeated hundreds of times over the next two years by total strangers. "Why hasn't this been done before? Why haven't we had a flag of our own?" That response, those words of reaction would be the refrain coming from people who thought it just didn't make sense that we had as a people never had a flag to display, carry, treasure, call our own. If confirmation had been needed from others of the value and worth of the flag, my cousin's reactions were just that and it was good to hear.

Gleason and I made a giant leap after that day. We decided to do our civic duty and let the President of the United States know what we had created. On June 28, 1967, we sent a letter to Lyndon Baines Johnson, announcing the "First Original Negro American flag". By July 4th, we had prepared similar letters for mailing to every Senator and Congressman. In each was enclosed a small photograph; in each we asked for endorsement of it. We mailed these letters in the absolute faith that our sincere efforts to announce something of special meaning to black people, even the small handful who knew about it, would be received in the spirit in which they were sent.

We haunted the post office to the point that the guys there got to know us by name and in a way to share our dejection when we came away empty-handed as often was the case. But, in late July, there was an envelope from 'The White House', dated July 20, 1967. It contained a letter written by

Whitney Shoemaker, Assistant to the President and read, in part:

> You know from the record of the last
> several years how devotedly the President
> had worked to obtain equal justice and
> equal opportunity for all citizens.
> These are the rights of all. No sector
> of the population can claim a greater
> share that the other. Yet each group
> among us can derive special pride from
> its own history and traditions. This
> right, too, is of equal value.

We seized on that sentence- "...each group among us can derive special pride from its own history and traditions". It seemed to say to us -- proceed, keep moving forward -- despite the lack of endorsement that was the essence of the letter.

We had moved forward. By the time this letter arrived we had ordered the making of eleven mint flags from a company in Verona, New Jersey. Later we discovered that the company made flags on order for many nations. Our little banner was just one more piece of business for them; they could not have known how important it was to us. Delivery of the mint flags came just in time for the Second National Black Power Conference held in Newark, beginning July 25th. We were about to make our first face-to-face presentation of the flag to our peers, black people trying to swim out of the turbulent waters of oppression we found ourselves fighting in the late 1960's.

Newark, in July of 1967, was a stricken city. The summer's heat and the fires of riots had not cooled when black people gathered at the Robert Treat Hotel. The city was still in a near state of siege. State troopers were everywhere; plainsclothes police were plainly marked and obvious. It was a time when one needed to have urgent business to travel into the city, and every moment there was marked by an insistent inner voice telling you to get out as soon as your business was over and done.

It seemed to us that it was some special strength or maybe it was a kind of arrogance and defiance that marked the gathering of people for the workshops and speeches and meetings over those three days. We sensed the urgency that registered in voices and the hasty movements of delegates.

We were looking at a microcosm of the civil rights movement in the confines of the churches and rooms where the delegates gathered.

The amalgam of black people in attendance at that conference reflected the range of interests, concerns and agendas that marked the leadership of the time. There were genuinely concerned representatives of black interests from every section of the country. They spoke in earnest voices in workshops, in gatherings around the sofas in the hotel lobby, in booths in the restaurants. Their every waking minute seemed spent trying to define what black power was and then to determine how best to steer it into the most effective course of action. They grappled with the realities of poverty, inadequate education, insulting work opportunities, poor housing, and all the ills afflicting the black mainstream. They seemed to find no easy answers to the questions they raised. Some of the questions were not heard too well above the din from the microphones as one "leader" after another rose to add his voice to the rhetoric that would make the papers the next day. Everybody, among the leaders, had a philosophy that was the ultimate in prescriptions for the problems of black people in this land of freedom and justice and plenty. Some revived the shade of Marcus Garvey and urged a return to Africa as the only right and reasonable course of action. Others proclaimed their leasehold on the soil of this country and their willingness to die to get their hands on the deed to that soil. Some were concerned with clarifying black identity, with trying to define what made black people truly black people. Some were anti-white; others militantly black. Some were casual onlookers; some didn't seem to give a damn what went down; it was important only to have been on this particular scene. And some were there to rip off the conference.

It was no place for political neophytes like Gleason and myself to make ourselves heard. Our only agenda was to announce the flag and get whatever endorsement, support, or encouragement we could. We ran into unexpected competition.

On the afternoon of the first conference day we put a flag on display on a table. It was one of the mint flags and this was the first public showing of the banner.

A woman came over to the table, looked disdainfully over the flag. She backed a few feet away from the table, planted her feet firmly then said, very loudly, that she knew two men over in Harlem who had designed a flag and she had brought it with her. Without hesitation, she whipped it out and started waving it around. It had a green field with a yellow border and some words written on it but she waved it so fast we couldn't see what the words were. While we craned to see the design, she began announcing at the top of her large voice, that this green flag should be the Negro flag. It was to fly from a school that was to be built soon in upstate New York. The opening of that school would take place sooner that scheduled if everybody at the conference would buy just one brick! Brick? Before anyone could digest that word, she opened her huge handbag and pulled out a yellow brick, held it up, and told everybody gathered around our table that she had bought a brick and wanted everyone there to buy one and if they would give her their names she would make sure they got a brick. She sold the invisible bricks. Right on the spot. Men were buying them . Right there.

I said to myself, "Mel, you ain't buying no brick from this crazy woman!" We weren't selling any, either.

When she finally hoisted sail and moved on to other groups in the lobby we concluded that we didn't have any real competition, after all. She was on the take, hauling in booty probably by the wheelbarrow full. Her appearance had startled us though and gave the first conference evening an unpleasant flavor, at least for us.

The next day was not unpleasant; it was chaotic.

Early in the session an emergency meeting was announced for the auditorium of a nearby church. Everyone picked up; the whole conference moved to that church. Once inside, the people were told of ominous rumors: the Newark Police and the State Police were coming, they were armed, they were walking down the street toward us at that very moment. A riot was about to start!

The police did come. Their guns were out.

The confusion was incredible. Tension was palpable as people tried to sort truth from rumor and tried to get a sense of what should be done in those moments before whatever was going to happen did happen. Flashbulbs went off, leaders huddled, people gathered their courage around themselves and prepared for the siege. It didn't come. The crisis ended. Groups broke apart as the need to find strength in numbers dissipated. The whole thing was unreal.

It was more unreal that later the papers insinuated that this had been a Conference-maneuvered and prescribed state of confusion. That defied belief. Could anyone deliberately instigate rumors of an impending riot or an unprovoked attack on the conference delegates just to secure publicity and media coverage? We chose not to believe that.

We listened to the leaders for the balance of that day. We heard the NAACP denigrated, the Urban League called a "white wash". It was business as usual as the agendas surfaced from those of prominence. We listened to Rap Brown, LeRoi Jones and civil rights personalities and community leaders present their points of view. When pauses came between sessions, we moved as close as we could to introduce ourselves and explain why we were there. We met disinterest, overwhelming disinterest, when we talked hurriedly about pride and unity behind a standard that could represent all the divergent views just as the Stars and Stripes sheltered a cauldron full of people, heritages, private interests and disparate views on everything from economic theories to religious convictions to the length of women's skirts.

When we could get no ear from the leaders, we turned to others, the less vocal people representing constituencies as diverse as black people are. In a couple of workshops we were given a few minutes to talk about the flag, to tell small groups of people about the colors, the symbols, what the flag meant to us, what we believed it could mean to all black people. Some souls seemed touched. Individually some people gave us quiet encouragement. We were never able to get to the point of asking for endorsement or support. We would not have gotten it if we had asked. There were too many agendas, too much rhetoric, too many people in a state of confusion about where the movement was going to endorse a symbol of a unified people. It almost seemed as though we were swimming across the currents of a mighty river; we didn't know which way the water was flowing, we knew only that the river was polluted. To get where we wanted to go we knew we had a lot of work to do -- and on our own.

We took with us, as we left the conference, the one clear consensus that was reached. No longer would we call ourselves "Negroes"; we were "black" and proud of it!

We also took with us a frustrating awareness of the rampart confusion among black leaders, as we saw it. The civil rights movement lacked clarity of purpose, lacked focused energy, was devoid of answers to the enormous problems faced by our people. For the next several weeks Gleason and I did nothing to promote awareness of the existence of the flag. It seemed more urgent in our frequent meetings to try and assess the state of being we felt characterized the movement.

We talked about the men who personified the most obvious lines of thought within the black community. Martin Luther King's dream was of brotherhood. His medium lay in the streets. His repose was on the hard mattresses of jails. His source of illumination was in the deep roots of the black church. His words flowed in the rhythms of the lined hymns of the childhoods through which we had passed.

Malcolm X was dead, assassinated. Searing thoughts and vibrantly voiced words that pierced the gut had been stilled. His dream was of black manhood asserting power. His medium was the word. His illumination seemed born in the north of Africa where Moslem fierceness of spirit met and melded with African loyalty to the tribe and people. His words were intense, magnified by the light reflected from the glasses at his eyes, forcing you to take the inner step to find where your manhood lay dormant, to awaken it and then to take what was your right

Adam Clayton Powell was in Washington, making his waves lap at the edges of the still waters of Congress. The New Frontier had been replaced with the Great Society and we black people were still poor, undereducated, uneremployed and feeling neither new nor great. Powell made magic with his voice too. His dream was of making the team and changing the style of play, giving the game the vitality of the street dressed in the uniform of Madison Avenue. His medium was in the hallowed halls of Congress during the week and the pulpit on the weekend. His repose was in the comfortable surroundings of one accustomed to living well. His source of illumination lay in an understanding of what power really was and the subtle and even devious ways it was exercised.

We talked about the NAACP and its measured pace toward its goals. It seemed such a torturous path to seek a birthright through the courts or in the Urban League's wedge maneuvers into corporate boardrooms.

There was something for everyone in the civil rights movement. You could match your action style to the rhythms of the church or the courts or the Congress. Or, you could hit the streets and the lunch counters or loot and riot out of frustration, anger and bitterness.

We talked about our children and the new times they faced as desegregation added a "d" to the abc's. The innocent young were to be fed like grain into an educational grist mill that was supposed to spew out uniform leveled flour for baking a new All-American pie. Desegregation was going to level us upward!

Most black people we knew talked about these things, talked in the deep idioms of our culture around the TV sets in their homes, sitting on the edges of their chairs as night cloaked their words. They talked about racism, oppression, the ghetto, men who moved and did things that shook the screens with reverberations of their actions. Rarely did those we knew do more than talk. Even more rarely did they reveal in the daylight the anger that had been in the words spoken in the dark of night. Black people were preparing to take advantage of the benefits that the Great Society promised. Many of them seemed to be affiliating themselves with the newest movement in the late 1960's, -- "I'm going to get all I can and the hell with you." For most of those people, we knew, it was most important that they pack away their anger and resentment as they learned the language of grant applications, deciphered the legalese of forms required to get some of the newly emerging monies, blood monies, that corporations and foundations were willing to share in the name of humanitarianism.

Despite the sense of standing apart from those whose haste was toward the treasure stores of the grantors, we believed still that there was an undercurrent of feeling among some young, black adults with whom we could identify. This group was composed of men and women in their late twenties who were beginning to make it in the workplace, who were buying modest homes, driving affordable cars, raising children in two-parent families, mowing the lawn on the weekend, quietly active in some community work, paying respect to parents (asserting our adulthood and independence while we did it). We were beginning to find a place for ourselves, by ourselves. No marches, no jails, no looting, no rioting. We were buying into a group for whom the dreams were beginning to come true. We thought, we believed, that we stood in the mid-ground with this group, somewhere between the helpless and oppressed and those whose grasp had far exceeded our reach.

We expected to be able to plant a symbol of pride in self, in our people, in our race, in the soil of this country and watch it gain acceptance and recognition. Surely those whose labors were producing some fruits could understand the depth of pride in self about which we were talking.

Our long evenings of discussions were coming to an end with the waning of the summer months. We had not solved the riddle of the confused and confusing agendas of the many designated and self-proclaimed leaders in the civil rights movement. We had no more easy answers than they to the massive problems our people faced. We did have a symbol of our hopes and of a fundamental pride we felt black people ought to show and so, in September, we began the process of reaching out to the public in earnest.

We sent letters of introduction, including a picture of the flag, to each Governor of the fifty states. Once again, we wrote to the White House, this time sending one of the mint flags. It was a small package; the flags were only 3' x 5' and they looked good. The little box carried a lot of hope with it to Washington and a letter saying simply that we wanted the President to have a mint flag.

In October we received our only response from a governor. North Carolina's Dan K. Moore responded through an administrative assistant, acknowledging and thanking us for the letter and photograph of the "First Original Negro American Flag". The assistant wrote "The Governor appreciates your giving him the opportunity to see this representation of this flag and the explanation of its symbols". That was it. One Governor responded. We never received even a postcard from the governor of our state.

It was not until December that the White House acknowledged receipt of the mint flag. This time the letter came over the signature of a personal Secretary to the President and thanked us for sending the flag. Though we knew Lyndon Johnson had not dictated the letter personally, we were pleased over one sentence:

> "He appreciated your thoughtfulness in
> remembering him in this symbolic way and
> commends each of you for the spirit of
> patriotism and pride you have in our
> beloved country."

These words were encouraging. By the time this letter arrived, however, the fruits of going public were appearing on a lot of branches. Lyndon Johnson's letter was just one of thousands we were beginning to receive. The flood of mail came in the wake of several steps we had decided to take beginning in September 1967. The first two steps appeared to be necessary, vital to the protection of the flag and of ourselves. Little did we expect the first step to influence so strongly those we involved in the second step.

Protection, we thought, meant we needed to incorporate ourselves if for no other reason than to move the flag under an umbrella separate from our personal resources --- our homes, cars and modest bank accounts. Should any legal problems arise these could be directed to GLEAMEL Enterprises,Ltd., the name we put on the incorporation papers.

The next step was to seek actively to organize a group of people to help promote awareness of the flag. We believed that if people knew about the existence of the flag, recognition and acceptance would follow like night after day. This we believed despite our experiences at the Black Power Conference and the mixed response we had received there. We rationalized to ourselves that the conference had had to contend with so many issues that seemed more pressing than adopting a symbol of unity and that only the timing of our appearance with the flag had resulted in the lack of recognition and positive response we had gotten from the group. It seemed to us that it was possible to reach out to the general public and secure the acceptance we felt the flag deserved. We were ready to welcome any ideas and assistance we could get to start moving in a concerted way toward awakening the general black community to the news of the flag.

We each called up a couple of people, friends we thought close enough to broach the concept. The first meeting was short and to the point. We wanted them to know what the flag meant to us and why we had designed it. We indicated that we wanted to expand, broaden the scope of efforts to make the country aware of it. The group was enthusiastic as we had hoped. The whole evening was upbeat and positive. Probably the most important words we could have heard were repeated over and over --- "Why did you keep this good thing to yourselves for so long?" It wasn't easy to tell then that we thought the idea so significant and in a way, so awesome, that we just couldn't share it easily. We didn't know what to expect when we approached the real world of the man in the street so we had taken the route of writing letters to distant public figures and gotten limited response. We had touched the edges of the "leadership" and encountered what looked like disinterest in return. What would happen when we went grassroots?

We found out at the next meeting.

The first group was enlarged to include a couple of lawyers, an accountant, and other people from the community we thought would and could help. There were nine of us sitting this time to discuss the awareness campaign we wanted to launch. Gleason's agenda and mine was to develop a plan for action to publicize the flag. Within minutes we discovered that most people in the group wanted to know what their "share" would be.

"Share?" Of what? Nobody wanted to take shares in the out-of-pocket costs that only Gleason and I had borne up to that point. There was no sales campaign, there was nothing to sell. We had two design mock-ups, one design banner, eleven mint flags (minus the one I sent to President Johnson), a patent and papers of incorporation. If anybody knew that money was involved we did. Money was needed to develop a real campaign and everything, so far, had been at our personal expense. Our purpose, we told them, was not to organize a group to make money. We wanted to generate ideas about how to make the flag reach into hearts and minds, but not pockets. There was no money to be made. Period.

The meeting ended soon and sourly. A couple of fellows lingered, talking out in front of my house, still wanting to know what their share would be. It was hard to absorb that kind of mentality and Gleason and I were surprised and hurt by the reaction we got. After everyone left, we decided to call each one and let them know that if it infringed on their time to work on this for free, then we'd let them know when we would have something to offer them.

One man decided to stay with us and work in a public relations capacity. John worked with us for several months offering ideas and doing legwork. He seemed to be the only one who understood that a patent and an incorporated entity were only the protection for an idea and not the golden doors leading to some quick-rich future.

Gleason and I continued to hold our usual daily meetings at the lunch hour. Sandwiches, cups of tea, and concentrated talk about the flag and how we might be able to generate interest in it made the mid-day hour go very quickly. In one of those meetings, we decided to get in step with the new use of the word "black" and so the flag became the Black American Flag. Shortly after that change, the idea developed that was to give the flag its first real publicity.

It was such a simple idea; we could not have foreseen the ripples that would result from casting this idea into the stream of our community's life.

United Nations Day was approaching. Flags of all nations and peoples would be flying with fanfare everywhere. Why not ask to have the Black American Flag placed atop a pole at the City Hall in the town where we lived!

Why not? We were homeowners, paid taxes, and had the right to go to City Hall and make a request.

We mapped out a strategy. We would go to the Mayor, tell him what we wanted, get his reaction and watch everything fall into place.

I had access to the Mayor. For several months I had served as chairman of the city's Human Relations Committee and knew him on more than a nodding basis. Getting an appointment to see him should be easy and it was.

Gleason and I arranged to get off work early to meet a few minutes before the mid-afternoon appointment. We found a coffee shop near City Hall, had a soda or two and talked about what we thought the meeting would be like. The cold sodas added some twinges to our stomachs, exarcerbating the nervousness over what we were about to try. We walked to City Hall slowly, still talking, and as we neared the steps Gleason said, as he often did, "This is history now, brother". My response, as usual, was to agree that it was, but, "Let's see how it works out". We knew that the Mayor was in his first term and had received great support from the black community. We believed that the timing was good. The nature of the working relationship I had with him seemed an additional positive factor which we expected to result in an encouraging response to our request.

We walked into City Hall, went to the Mayor's Office. The secretary, crisp but pleasant, knew me and told us to have a seat, that the Mayor would be with us in a few minutes. We used the time to sit quietly, each of us thinking our own separate thoughts as we tried to calm ourselves for the meeting. In a short time we were ushered into the large room, nicely laid out with old-fashioned heavy furniture. The room was spit-and-polish clean, old woods gleaming. There was an aura of power, security, authority in the room and its furnishings. The Mayor, a young man, patient and handsome, was curious about our purpose for being there. Any white mayor, facing an appointment with black residents of his city at their request in the late 1960's, was bound to be very concerned about what brought them there. That may have been what prompted us to wear white shirts and ties and not dashikis. We were not going in to make waves; we wanted only to unfurl a flag. The militant nationalism of the dashiki was not what we wanted to present. We wanted to talk up an idea.

We got right down to it.

I told him that Gleason and I were there to discuss with him something we had created, that we had worked on it for quite some time, that we thought on United Nations Day it could be unfurled on a pole outside City Hall in Linden in honor of Black Americans.

The words flew out, giving the Mayor no time to respond or even interrupt. It was urgent to say it all, sell him with the power of our belief in the rightness of giving black residents of the city a sense of pride without violence. All we wanted was to have the flag on display at City Hall on United Nations Day.

He slumped in his chair. He sat silent, stunned, eyes glazed. For a long moment there was silence in the room before he cleared his throat, pulled himself upright in his chair, put his hands on the edge of the desk, and started stalling.

"It's very interesting what you men have done. Without a doubt it's a surprise to me. But, I don't have the right at this point to say what is unfurled on the flagpole out there. I can't take that liberty. What I can suggest to you is that you will have to take this before City Council. You can write a letter and I'll have it placed on the agenda. If it is placed on the agenda they have to read it and have to react to it."

He sat back after that, tension still filling his body. He looked at us carefully, measuring our reactions to his words. He slumped again when I opened my brief case and pulled out a letter. It was passed over to him with a few words."We thought that might be the process so we brought a letter with us."

He reached for it, read it, and said, "All I can say is that I'll do my part and that is to make sure they get it for the agenda tomorrow night."

We thanked him, told him we appreciated his time and what he was doing for us and that we would come back to Council meeting and see what they had to say.

We stood up, shook hands, walked to the door. He stopped there, recovered enough to make small talk about the Human Relations Committee and how it was coming. I told him that I hoped to have a progress report soon and that the committee was made up of fine people, aggressive people who had arrived at good rapport with each other. It was true; the committee seemed about to tackle some of the serious problems of the community.

Gleason didn't say anything until we got outside the building. Then he said, "I think we shocked him with what we had." My response was, "I think we shocked the stuffing out of him but he handled it very well." We agreed that we had to show up the next night to see what would happen at Council meeting. We went our separate ways to tell our wives about the results of the appointment with the Mayor. As usual though, he and I wound up talking at his house later that evening. His living room was small, serene in blue and white. It was a good place to be to generate ideas, to do quite thinking that preceded action. Whenever we got ready to come to grips with events we somehow wound up in my basement. Maybe it was the posters on the wall, especially the one with the black Santa Claus "dreaming of a black Christmas", that gave us the steam to do whatever the moment required.

The first words about the flag were spoken in Gleason's living room; the first flag was begun in my basement. It went like that for all the months he and I worked on this thing together; dream here, do it there.

We sat that evening and thought out loud about the two possible courses of action City Council might take. We considered briefly that they might not approve the idea. We discarded that notion. Surely no one would object to displaying the flag on United Nations Day. We concentrated instead on the good outcome we expected and planned to react quietly and with dignity when Council approved our request.

I plodded through the next day, keeping a corner of my mind focused on the importance of the meeting and my need to remain calm in anticipation of the outcome. We arrived there in good time, took seats about half way back in the solemn Council Chamber. We had plenty of time to look at the pictures on the walls, huge portraits of past mayors. Needless to say, they were all white as were the current Councilmen. Dead center of us hung a gigantic American flag. Facing us were eight chairs arrayed under that flag, empty and silent as was the room before people gathered slowly for the meeting.

The Councilmen moved into the room in little clusters of two or three, seated themselves with the look of boredom that passes for authority in a small town and proceeded into the usual matters that come before an urban community's politicians. At last, reference was made to a letter from two citizens requesting that a "flag" be unfurled and describing what the flag stood for. After the letter was read, the councilman representing our ward moved to table the decision in view of the need to have more time to "study the idea." I was not prepared for this decision. After a momentary pause, I looked at Gleason and saw that he was as stunned as I. While we sat gathering our thoughts, the meeting was coming to a close. There remained only that part of the evening when Council invited the audience to speak if anyone wished.

I was nervous as hell but rose anyway and went to a microphone at the front center of the chamber. There were about forty-five people scattered here and there in the room and they seemed ready to go home, but there was no way we could let the meeting end without pursuing the letter and the decision the council had made. I gave them my name, indicating that I was one of the designers of the flag, told them that we had heard our letter read and heard Council say the matter should be tabled. I asked what it meant to table it and why it had to be done and why we couldn't get a yes or no then and there. I took a breath and said we'd spoken to the Mayor about it and he had seemed to understand what our request was about. Finally, I told them that United Nations Day was a fitting day for such a display and asked what really was the position of the Council.

The Fourth Ward Councilman responded that since the NAACP had not endorsed it, they felt that they were not going to make a statement on the request at the time. I blew right out of control, shouting a question, wanting to know what the NAACP had to do with the request or the flag. It was important to tell the Council that they didn't want to hear from the NAACP or the Urban League when issues were raised by the black community, so it was impossible to understand why they needed that endorsement when all we wanted was to exhibit some pride in ourselves as a people.

The councilman said nothing. Gleason stepped up to the microphone immediately, explained that he too was a designer of the flag, had placed his name on the letter of request and that he was confused about the decision the Council had reached.

Our councilman responded that tabling it meant that they had not reached a final decision yet and hoped to make one soon. "How soon?" I shouted. "Why not this evening?" Suddenly the gavel came down. We were told our time was up. I asked once more for a decision, told them that we felt all we were getting was rhetoric and nothing else. The chairman hit the gavel on the table again.

We stood there for maybe twenty seconds then turned and walked back to our seats. Our city had really come through for us. Sure. Those eight chairs were occupied by some angry white folks who could not stand to hear the thoughts of citizens, could not stand to hear of the pride of black residents of the community.

We walked out, passing by the sergeant-at-arms at the door, feeling the cold and hostile look he gave us. Outside the Chambers, a newspaper reporter ran up to us, excited, talking fast. In all our quiet thinking the evening before, the possibility of newspaper coverage had not once been mentioned but this man smelled a story after sitting through the otherwise boring meeting and wanted us to talk with him. We stood there in the corridor, talked for a few minutes about our request and the flag and what it was and meant. He asked where he could get in touch. We gave him my telephone number and went home to wait and see whether he would call.

He did. He wanted us to come over to the office, bring a flag and tell him more about the whole thing. We grabbed a flag, drove to the Elizabeth

Daily Journal building in record time, and spent half an hour with that reporter.

We left there in a state of wonder at all the events of that one evening. We had expected a positive response from the City Fathers and had received nothing. We had not anticipated newspaper interest or coverage and that's exactly what we got. We had held onto an idea for close to eight months, sharing it with only a few friends and our families, making one public foray to the Black Power Conference, writing letters shotgun over the country. We had found supportive reactions from families, avarice in friends, disinterest among the black leadership, silence from nearly everyone we had written. One simple request made to City Council blew the flag right to the top of the page.

It was the next day when I realized the full extent of what had happened the night before. My mother called early in the morning, excitedly telling me to turn on the radio because the news report was repeating every few minutes that two men had gone to City Council in Linden and asked to put up a black flag on United Nations Day and Gleason's name and mine were being given over and over. "Get the newspapers, too" she said, "You're on page three at the top!"

And there it was. The Newark paper, the Star Ledger, was carrying a small article in reference to the flag. Before the day was over we had begun to receive the first of hundreds of telephone calls from friends and even more heartening, a call from the Newark Evening News asking to send a photographer to get its own story. He arrived; we stood beside the design flag in my basement for a picture and the next day there was an extensive article in the News. The Elizabeth Journal came back the following day for an even longer article.

We felt good! Things were beginning to happen. The flag was on its way out to the world.

Chapter 3

Mail started filling the heretofore empty box in Roselle. The men in the Post Office were as excited as we and would call out to us as we entered the building, "Hey, man, its full!" The letters spoke of pride; they came from old, young, women, men and children. One woman wrote especially about her pride in finding that someone else had taken the time to demonstrate theirs. One youngster in Newark wrote that he had shed tears to discover that there were black men who could design a flag that **we** could exhibit with pride. His was a short letter and a good one. It was important to us to see proof that our children read the papers, knew how to write a letter, and could express themselves about the way they felt.

In a matter of days we had received a couple hundred letters. We were so inundated with them that we could do no more than read them, pile them up, tie down the package and hope that at some point in the future we could respond to those people who had taken the time to write to us. One letter in particular gave us a tremendous feelings of accomplishment. Somehow the local stories had wound up in the "Stars and Stripes" and black servicemen in Vietnam wrote asking for flags.

This letter made us realize that we had so little in the way of materials we could share with people who were asking for flags, descriptions and information. It was time to start putting together a brochure, get small flags made up, maybe even decals of the flag. Gleason and I, with John decided to begin to package something that would answer the requests we were receiving.

We spent several evenings developing a small foldover brochure we thought expressed the reasons why we had designed the flag and described the symbols and colors in detail. It seemed appropriate also to order small decals that might be put on a car or wherever one wanted. That was the easiest of the materials to decide on and when an acquaintance mentioned that he had a printing press we were rolling.

We dropped by the man's shop one evening. It was located on a run-down block of small black-owned businesses housed in narrow store fronts under tenement apartments. The shop was cluttered with piles of new and used printing paper. The man had one press sitting under a 75-watt bulb hanging at the end of a cord. The walls were dirty grey and the paint was peeling. As we looked around we wondered if he could do the job. He was a homeboy though, so we had to give him a try. I handed him the block print I had made. He said he could produce the decals for a very small price so we left there jubilant in expectation that we could get the sample decal the very next weekend. When we saw the sample we were not happy. The colors just weren't right, not what my eye for color said they should be. Gleason was of the opinion though, that while we could do better elsewhere, this was a start and that we should go ahead and order the first full set. We did. He had captured the design accurately enough.

We were promised delivery for the next Wednesday at 9:00 p.m. Promptly at that hour, we picked them up. It felt good to have that one box of 500 decals, six by eight inches, the diagonals, sword and wreath in place, and the words "Black American Flag" in bold letters at the bottom. Within hours we were passing them out to anyone who asked for one. Also within hours, the police raided the print shop. At 1:00 a.m. following our pick-up of the decals, the FBI collected the man and his press. He was printing some of the worst counterfeit money ever seen!

The decals had been easy to plan; the brochure was not. We spent a long time, many evenings discussing the statement that would accurately describe the origin, meaning, and purpose of the flag. It was essential to make clear that the purpose was to establish within Black Americans a unity of nationality and a pride in history and tradition that we had not had since arriving in this country in chains hundreds of years before. Ultimately the statement made reference to the many wars fought in and by this country to bring liberty and justice to many peoples and lands, and reminded the reader that Black Americans were without commemorative holidays, nationally recognized heroes, or most important, an acknowledged place in American history.

The final draft of the statement was a strong one. It was a long statement, full of the sentiments that impelled us to do what we had done--- establish a point of   pride for Black Americans in the face of what we perceived as failure on the part of the power structure, white and black, the school systems, and even black people themselves, to fulfill the mandate for equal citizenship, recognition of accomplishments, justice, liberty, and the pursuit of happiness in this country of ours. It was intended to be a call to black people to rise, like the phoenix, from the ashes of slavery, the agony of caricatures and stereotypes, the self-destruction of rioting and looting, and the horrors of assassinations and senseless death. Rise, rise in spirit, rise in commitment to the struggle for equal justice and human dignity under the constitution, rise in pride in self that did not require processed hair, self-denigration, or flinching from the word "black".

The back page of the foldover contained the final touch to our hours of work, a short pledge:

> I pledge my respect to the flag of the Black
> American and to the people it represents. I shall
> remain aware of the color red, being ever mindful
> that it represents the blood shed by our forefathers.
> The color black gives me pride and identity. I shall
> always remain true to the American ideal that all men
> are created equal.

With this pledge we wrapped up the brochure. And, we found another printer to do the job for us.

It seemed incredible that only a couple of weeks had gone by since the City Council meeting. The newspaper coverage had started to move us into a pattern of life that would affect us in some very powerful ways. It would be an understatement to say that our lives changed. Everything changed. Our evenings, once spent with families, puttering around our homes, parties with friends, ordinary lives--changed. Reading bedtime stories to our daughters became hours of opening envelopes and absorbing the scribbled words that hundreds of unknown Black Americans were sending to us. Hours that might have gone to checking the storm windows, cutting the grass once more before winter arrived, or taking out the cameras for some pictures of October foliage, were spent instead in devising the brochure, trying to respond to telephone calls to come present the flag at a church group or civic meeting in the community.

Changes came at our jobs, too. Perhaps five days after the City Hall meeting, my employer came up to me at my workbench and after spending a few minutes talking about the display I was working on, edged into what he really wanted to talk about. He wanted to know why I had not said anything to him about what I had been doing. It seems that his friends knew I worked for him and he was embarrassed to tell them that he was completely in the dark about the flag. He thought I should have said something to him about it. My response to him was that I didn't think he would have understood what a flag for Negro Americans was all about. He shot back that I was wrong, he would have understood, and what is more, he could have shown me how to design it. That did It! It was easy then to tell him that I had not asked for help because I already had help, that it was no way right to ask him to aid in designing a flag for my people any more than he would have thought it was right to ask me to help him design one for his people. I couldn't understand why he thought I would seek help from him and told him so.

He was visibly upset by my response. He left the shop soon after our conversation that day, and for the rest of the months I remained there, the relationship was distant and cool.

Maybe this encounter with the reactions of a non-black with whom I worked closely should have told me something. Maybe that something was that control over the lives and actions of black people was not going to be given up easily, with slavery over only one hundred years. Maybe the message was that the overriding belief was still that we did not possess the mentality, ability, or creativity to do something as original as what we had done--without his help. Maybe the message he wanted to convey was that we had no right to do it in the first place. I think, though, he came to understand me a little better after our conversation, enough so he kept his distance for the balance of my time there.

Gleason, too, experienced reactions of cold-shouldering and a cautious by-passing from people in his workplace. Almost as soon as our names first appeared in the papers we began to find that we were suspect in some way. Later this would surface in a number of ways that would cause us some concern, but for now we were riding the first movement of a tiny wave that was to wash us out of our commonplace lives into new and absorbing experience.

Each day following the first newspaper story on October 19, 1967, brought a full measure of unaccustomed activity--the groundswell of mail,

the many invitations requesting us to these activities and our need to prepare the brochure, secure decals and several sizes of flags to give away
while we kept a balance between work, family, and personal activities, gave
us little time to develop a strategy for placing the flag before the public.
For a couple of months we just rode the tide letting it take us where it
would. One of those places was a church group in Paterson, New Jersey.
This speaking engagement was one of the most unusual we would ever
experience.

Calls extending invitations to speak came to both of us, and we worked
out a plan to get lead information about the groups inviting us. We asked
John to follow up on initial calls and find out whatever he could about the
group. Having that kind of advance knowledge helped us develop the approach we would use in the presentation itself. Knowing we would be in
front of senior citizens made the butterflies rest easier in the stomach before leaving home. When the call came from Paterson, the pastor said he
read the story in the Newark paper and was very interested in having us
appear. He was most cordial and when John indicated that his sources gave
a "good as gold" recommendation, we geared up for the receptive audience
the pastor said we would have. I called Reverend Sanders back to tell him
we would be there. He was enthusiastic, anxious to have us, said he wanted
us to meet his wife and family and a few of his members a his apartment
and then go on down to the church for the program.

Gleason and I drove to Paterson carrying a mint flag and one of several
collapsible poles we had bought. This was going to be one of our first
contacts with an audience at some distance from the Linden area and we
eagerly looked forward to this presentation.

We arrived at the address, a neat, small, brick apartment house. We took
the elevator to Reverend Sanders' apartment on the second floor and knocked
on the door. Immediately it flew open. Reverend Sanders stood there, short
and pudgy, with a huge smile on his face. He greeted us, "I know who you
are", flung the door wide and said, "Come on in, come right on in!"

It was not a fashionable apartment. A few pieces of sturdy furniture
lined the walls and six people sat around the dining room table in almost
frozen positions. He told us to have a seat, that he would be right back with
us. The people were very quiet through his invitation to us. We sat, gave the
group a pleasant greeting, spoke about the weather and how good it was to
be there. Their responses were murmured and guarded. I wondered whether the absence of the Reverend had anything to do with that. The thought

had barely crossed my mind when he walked back into the dining room wearing a blue sharkskin suit with a white-on-white shirt. His smile lit up the room; so did the after-shave lotion he has splashed on his face!

He beamed as he stood there radiating a charm that seemed both roguish and intriguing. The people began to smile a little as they warmed up in the presence of the pastor. He planted his feet apart and started the most amazing speech.

"I want you to know you boys are gon' down in history 'cause you gon' be the biggest in the world. Everybody's gon' know about you. This is gon' be the greatest thing that gon' happen to black folks. This is a banner that will lead us on to bigger and better things."

We hear "Amen,Amen," coming from the people. The strength of their murmurs rose in intensity as his voice climbed. We knew this man had the church in his hands and that he was going to give us a tremendous boost before the congregation that night. He was still talking. "I want you to know that church is gon' start in a few minutes and I have the deacon here with the membership and he's gon' take you on down to the church and when you get there I know you want to have a few minutes to be by yourself. I'll be down in a few minutes myself."

He turned to a small man who immediately jumped up and smiled broadly. The Reverend went on, "Deacon, will you start the church for me 'cause I want you to know that not only are they gon' speak tonight, but we gon' have the Governor here at the church, and we gon' have some judges and some councilmen here at the church, and I'm gon' speak cause I'm a Democrat, and being a Democrat I want you to know that everything is gon' be right 'cause if we ain't Democrats we gon' really lose. So this is why we having this meeting tonight and that's why I want you all here with that flag cause' I'm gon' show the Governor!

Reverend Sanders rolled his words with the vigor and style I had heard all through my childhood. This man knew just when to lay power into his voice and when to bring it down to a whisper. He was getting the response he wanted from his listeners, their senses responding to the rhythms he pushed through their conscious minds to the inner recesses of their souls. We were all mesmerized but not enough to miss hearing him say that the Governor was to appear. I sat up. This was going to be great!

We picked up our coats and joined the group leaving the apartment, still awash in the words of the pastor who stood at the door as we headed for the elevator.

A feeling of jubilation and anticipation flowed through the crowded elevator as though there was some silent singing of "We're on Our Way to the Promised Land". The elevator dropped down past the first floor to the basement. The deacon said as the doors opened, "Here's the Church."

I looked out the elevator door. Coal was banked on a chute leaning up to a corner window. To the left a few folding chairs stood in neat rows. Above them two naked light bulbs strung from the ceiling. This was the church! It was in the cellar in a coal bin. He had gotten us there to present the flag to the church of six members sitting on folding chairs under bare bulbs in a cellar. I couldn't believe it. Laughter started rumbling inside me and it was just about to burst loose. I went behind the coal chute, bent over, and held my sides to keep from exploding in nervous guffaws. Gleason followed me, his eyes dulled with disbelief. It took several moments before we could speak. We stood and shook our heads silently. Finally, we agreed there were six people out there who were ready to listen to us if the Governor arrived--which we very much doubted now--that would be good. We could go ahead and make our presentation in this basement and that would be better. Gleason gave a wry smile and moved out with me to where the bulbs were hanging. We strung the flag between two pipes as the congregation settled down in their seats. Just as we finished, Reverend Sanders walked in singing, "What a Friend We Have In Jesus." Everybody joined in. The cellar rang with the sound of true belief, the Reverend's voice leading us affirming the faith that black people have hung onto for generations.

The hymn ended and he motioned us to sit. He wasted not time correcting the information he had given us upstairs.

"We have some honorable guests with us here tonight and since the Governor is not here and you know we all Democrats here tonight, we gon' start the service. See, if we ain't Democrats we ain't gon' do nothing in this town."

My mind raced, "You ain't going to do nothing is right, Democrat or no, cause this ain't nothing. You in a cellar, man; you in a coal bin."

He turned his smile to us and beckoned us to stand beside him and begin. We talked for fifteen minutes about the flag, explaining it in words that would become as familiar to us as our names. We spoke of the design, the symbols, the colors, the deeper meaning of what we felt the flag represented. We ended with the pledge, feeling the quiet, intent and attentive air of our listeners, their heads nodding as we told them of the urgency of displaying pride in self and race.

We took down the flag, apologized for not being able to stay to meet the Governor and left.

When we got to the car we laughed. It had not been easy to keep a straight face when we entered that basement; the relief at being out of there made us give in to more nervous laughter. When we were finally over the worst of our response to this experience, we agreed that John had not done his job. If his sources had really been "as good as gold", he might have better warned us.

We talked for a few minutes before pulling away from the apartment building. We reminded each other that black churches were to be found in storefronts, second floors of funeral parlors and private homes. Imposing structures, large and small, held the Sunday prayer meetings for our people. We should have been able to accept this as just another of the large variety of forms in which black people gathered for worship. But the caricature of a minister that Reverend Sanders presented and the solemn acceptance of him by his congregation were so incongruous, we reacted with laughter. We should have cried for the poverty of spirit and pride that drove those people into a cellar. We could only hope that we left them something that could raise their aspirations a little higher.

We were solemn when I made a U-turn and headed out of Paterson. Before we left that city, though, purely by accident we found a larger and more satisfyingly real audience.

A short block or two from Reverend Sanders' "church", we noticed a number of people entering an old automobile showroom decked out with signs advertising a poverty program meeting. Politicians' faces smiled from posters as large groups of people hurried down the street toward the building. I stopped the car and we looked in and saw an audience of black people. It was ready made for us. We'd been duped once that evening and there was no point in going home when there was a huge group of people who might want to hear what we had to say. Gleason was hesitant, remarking that we had no invitation to go in and there might be trouble. I urged him to take a chance with me; we couldn't do worse that we had already experienced. He agreed. We put the pole together, hung the flag, and I walked right into the room with it. Somewhere a voice said, "Hey, there's the boys with the flag. There's the Black American Flag." I kept walking right up to the front of the room. A man met me with a smile on his face. I told him I wanted just a few words with the audience. He said, "You got it, brother." He sat me next to a white judge on the makeshift stage. The judge blanched but stayed put.

He even made it through his speech without revealing the inner turmoil his face had shown as I sat beside him. He stayed through our presentation, too. He didn't run.

I talked for only a few minutes. The audience was receptive beyond belief, jumping to their feet, applauding and crowding up to ask for flags, anything we might have to give them. We had nothing with us, nothing to leave with them except the sense of what the flag meant.

The man who had greeted me as we came in told us to come back "anytime." He said he could always get a crowd for us and that he wanted to work with us.

We left. Paterson had been a good place to visit after all. Trenton was not.

In late November 1967, Gleason called to tell me that we had an invitation from a minister in Trenton who not only wanted to buy a flag, but also had gotten in contact with a local newspaper that wanted to do a story about us and the flag. All he wanted from us was a date to make a presentation at his church. It sounded very promising and we looked forward to driving down to meet the minister and to setting a date.

When we arrived in Trenton and located Reverend Martin's house, we were impressed with the calm, purposeful manner he exhibited. He had a large family, five boys, and they seemed awed by the flag. We spent a heartwarming two hours with Mr. Martin, his family, and the reporters from the Trenton Chronicle, who came to take photographs and a story for the Sunday paper. It was agreed that we would return on the Sunday following the news release to appear before the full church.

The drive home seemed short. We were excited about this opportunity to return to Trenton and talked about it incessantly on the way home.

On Tuesday following the Sunday edition of the paper, we received clippings of a very detailed article. It was well-written and included an invitation to the public to attend the services at the church to see the flag first hand. We were elated. The article was a treasury of information about the flag.

Thursday the bottom dropped out. Reverend Martin called Gleason and in a very brief conversation begged him not to come back to Trenton. When Gleason asked why, the minister replied that he had received many threatening notes and letters from people who were willing to burn down the church with everyone in it if we came back with the flag. His family had been threatened; their lives were on the line. Gleason told me that he could almost feel the terror and panic in the man's voice.

We did not go. There was no point in going to a place where there was fear. There was no point in precipitating violence by the presentation of a non-violent symbol of pride.

The Trenton experience was unusual in the depth of anguish generated by mention of the flag. We must have appeared before churches, civic groups and clubs more than seventy times between mid-October and early January 1968. Most meetings ended in a swell of enthusiasm and genuine interest in the flag. People wanted to buy flags and decals. They eagerly took the brochures to read at leisure. They displayed the flag in barber-shops, Mom and Pop stores, beauty parlors, churches, meeting halls. De-cals latched on to bumpers and windows by the hundreds. We felt that the little man enjoyed this means of making a statement of pride to those who could see the flags and decals.

We usually went together to speaking engagements. We always ended with the two of us holding the flag for a final moment in which the audi-ence could absorb the colors and symbols. These audiences nearly always responded with encouraging words to us to continue to carry a message of hope, pride and accomplishment. Except the response in Trenton, we nev-er came face to face with open denial during those first few heady months.

It was a hectic time for us. We averaged four meetings during the week and sometimes four on the weekend. The enthusiastic responses we re-ceived energized us. It was deeply gratifying to discover the interest that prompted groups to invite us and the warmth of their reaction to the flag itself.

We sometimes heard words of caution, especially from older members of audiences. One man in particular thought we were doing something very important and that we would become targets for the vicious who would find some means to silence us. We listened patiently but we were young and strong in our belief. Fear did not walk beside us. What had we to fear when we spoke only truth and meant only to generate pride through a sym-bol? We had no grand strategy to overturn the society; we were not a new wave of revolutionaries; we had no intention of usurping the role of civil rights leaders. We wanted only to do what we were doing--trying to make others aware of a history and a heritage that were magnificent. There was so much pride to acknowledge of our own worth. That was the message we took to audiences wherever we went. That was the message we had intend-ed to give in Trenton.

October '67 to January '68 had been busy. News articles appeared, letters arrived by the hundreds, appearances absorbed all our time. We received a letter from Lyndon Johnson acknowledging receipt of the flag; Nathan Wright accepted a mint flag before the Men's Club of St. Augustine Church in Elizabeth and expressed deep pleasure at its existence. Occasionally radio stations mentioned the flag and an extraordinary honor was paid to our hometown, Linden.

> Members of the Army's 25th Division in Vet Nam
> Have voted Linden the "City of the Year", according
> to word received this week in a letter to Mayor John
> T. Gregorio, from a staff sergeant in the outfit.

On January 10, 1968, the letter containing this news had been sent to the Mayor in care of the *Linden Leader*. The men of the division had read the article which appeared in the *Stars and Stripes* following the rejection of our plea to City Council back in October. We had received a letter from them earlier, expressing their congratulations to us as designers of the flag, and their request for a small flag, a request we quickly honored. It was particularly ironic that the letter signalling the division's recognition of the city was sent to the Mayor and that he then had to forward it to us. It must have left a bitter taste in his mouth to have to acknowledge an honor received as a result of a denial to citizens in that town. What he probably did not sense was the greater irony that the honor came from black men fighting an unholy war in an alien land for a country which had yet to recognize the blood shed by hundreds of thousands of black men in more honorable wars for more just causes.

We took pride in releasing the letter to the newspaper and once again seeing that recognition of the flag.

Other acknowledgments came. Some reviews of the flag were positive; some were sidestepping masterpieces. The Chairman of the Commission on Human Rights for The City of New York thanked us for our descriptive information about the "First Original Negro Standard Banner" and he went on to express his sentiments that "... significant measures within the framework of our already structured society, to vastly improve basic living conditions for Negroes..." was something that he strongly supported. We thought he had read our letter urging pride in a race of people as a call for economic progress above all.

Ralph Bunche wrote to thank us for our letter and the photograph of the "First Original Negro National Flag". He said it was "... an attractive emblem, but (he) did not favor the idea of a separate flag for any ethnic group". Edward R. Brooke thought, ..."objectives sought through the creation of a Negro National Flag are indeed commendable, but (he) wonder(ed) if these are best achieved in this symbolic manner." Brooke wrote that"... a flag has always been a symbol of recognition of a sovereign state or nation to which all the citizens therein owe some sort of allegiance." He was concerned that the flag might encourage the more militant segments in the civil rights movement toward complete separation of the Negro from the majority in this country. He therefore "... could not endorse the creation of the flag... despite its most worthy objectives."

Most of the mail we received came unsolicited. Whenever we sought endorsement via letters, we failed to receive it from those we thought in a position to give it with authority. Those whose sentiments were not solicited gave freely of their endorsement and their wholehearted support of the concept and the design. If the depth of feeling expressed by blacks who wrote to us be taken as signs of acceptance of the flag by our brothers, it would have been flying in every major city across the country. By January 1968 we had close to two thousand such letters. The mail bolstered our belief in the readiness of black people for this symbol, so we tried again to gain recognition of it from a city government which had a large black population. This time we chose Newark for a major unfurling at City Hall.

The experience in Linden had taught us that when confronted by a new element of the black community, the white power structure ran for cover to the old established black organizations. The City Council and Mayor had needed assurance that the NAACP. and the Urban League endorsed the flag before they could give any consideration to our request to fly it. We sought such an endorsement prior to approaching the Newark city government.

March was nearing and with it the observance of Crispus Attucks Day. Schools would be closed and there would be the annual parade later in the month. The impetus for these observances had come from the Crispus Attucks Society based in Newark. We thought endorsement from the Society would provide the old-line establishment support needed. We sought out the chairman and founder of the Society, John Thomas, in late January as we prepared to organize a neat package for Newark city government.

We met with Mr. Thomas one evening at his home. He struck us immediately as a man who could get things done. His impressive height and deep voice reinforced the air of command about him. We had copies of all the news articles, a stack of letters, a brochure, and a flag. We talked for a long time about our efforts our speeches, and the interest we were seeing and feeling. He nodded his head encouragingly as we talked, asked questions frequently, and was openly enthusiastic when we made two requests of him. We wanted endorsement of the flag by the Society and the assistance of the group in persuading the powers-that-be in Newark to fly the flag on March 5th, Crispus Attucks Day. He was firm in his response that he would do both. This was an important step for the flag. We were as eager to work with him and the organization he had founded as he was enthusiastic about the flag and what it represented.

When we left the meeting that night, we knew we had to write a formal letter requesting support of the Society and to make a presentation of a mint flag to the organization. More flags needed to be ordered because they might be carried in the Attucks Day Parade in late March. But first, it was important that we organize our letter of request to Newark City Hall as a simple but effective message. After this was done, we readied to go to Boston in early March, as Mr. Thomas had suggested, for the celebration of Crispus Attucks Day at the site where he had fallen with the first shots of the Revolutionary War. Things fell into place. All letters were written and plans were laid to go to Boston.

It was almost anti-climactic to receive word a day or two before leaving for Boston, that the flag had been displayed at a breakfast meeting of Negro Educators at the Waldorf-Astoria Hotel in New York City. This was, however, a very special recognition. Black educators held sway over the minds and attitudes of black children particularly during the crucial times of the late '60s. Their desire to display the flag was, to us, a good and positive sign of growing recognition. It was also a sign that the flag was moving out across the country and that people were beginning to display it in meaningful places without our request or even fore knowledge.

The letter of endorsement from the Crispus Attucks Society was received in good time. The Society, through Mr. Thomas, was pleased to accept a mint flag and to give wholehearted endorsement to the "First Official Flag to Represent Afro-Americans". Without haggling we received acknowledgment that the flag would be unfurled at Newark City Hall.

We were finally on our way --- to Boston and the observance of Crispus Attucks Day and then a return to Newark to see the flag flying at City Hall.

Knowing that a letter strongly endorsing the flag from the Society's founder had preceded us we expected the two days in Boston would be days of excitement and exhilaration. Neither of us had been there before; neither of us had imagined that we would make a trip to that city with so much support to encourage us. We were truly pleased to be going.

Boston, with its quaint cobblestone streets and skyscrapers--a mixture of old and new America -- caught our attention and interest immediately and seemed a paradox for us. We arrived on the evening of March 4th just in time for another dinner. The dining room was elegant: voices were subdued, black waiters in black uniforms, white towels draped precisely over their arms, an air of dedicated servitude about them hovered solicitously. I felt we were in some misbegotten plantation house, magically transformed into masters with willing slaves waiting on us hand and foot. Dinner was difficult to digest. Before long, the evening got even worse.

A woman from the Newark Attucks Society passed our table as we tried to enjoy the meal. John, who had accompanied us, spoke to her, introduced us and asked whether we might speak with her some time during that evening. We didn't understand the cool and disdainful "Yes," until later when we arrived at her door. She knew who we were and what we wanted to talk about and she was ready for us. She had gathered a small group of the Newark contingent around her and wasted no time when we sat down.

We had barely begun to thank the group for its support, when she cut us off. She let us know that she was aware of our conversations with Mr. Thomas about the flag and that we wanted to fly it in Newark on March 5th and that it was definite that "someone" had overstepped bounds. Mr. Thomas had been the culprit, encouraging us with a letter of endorsement, securing still another letter from the Boston Society, and promising support in the Newark effort. She was explicit that the rest of the Newark group didn't like the idea of any of this because they were "all Americans and wanted to stay Americans." Most of all, they saw "no need for a flag to be put up for black folks because black folks didn't need no black flag." They especially did not need a flag that "didn't have no ships, planes, or men with guns behind it." She sat back after delivering this with unaltering emphasis, letting the words linger in the air for effect, secure that she had put us in place.

Before we could gather words to explain to her that the flag had never been intended to represent a race of people preparing for war, a man seated at the side of the room put the issue into a far less martial context. He wanted to know how much money we had and whether we had thought of becoming partners with the Society in both the promotion of the flag and the profit from that promotion. He was clearly disappointed to hear that we had no money, we had nothing to give anybody and we were interested only in securing the Society's endorsement of the flag itself and its assistance in expanding awareness of what it represented. He dismissed us with clear disinterest and the throwaway remark that he didn't know how we were going to do any of that if we had no money. Since we had nothing to offer except and idea and commitment to it they had no intent to pursue the discussion further. We left, disgust rising in our throats.

In the lobbies of the hotel we found other people to whom we introduced ourselves and explained what we were about. Many were rank and file members of the Society whose skills in brokering were not yet in place. They talked with us about symbols of pride and asserting that pride in a tangible way without violence. Their earnestly spoken words reassured us. Gaining access to some receptive minds balanced our experience with the Newark contingent and made it easier to sleep in anticipation of the program to be held the next morning at the death site of Crispus Attucks.

March 5th was a cold yet clear day. We rode through the city noting the concentrated blend of preserved history in carefully tended old buildings and the tempered vibrancy of the '60s on campuses and in the faces of citizens going about their day. The buses took us finally to a set of cobblestones placed in a circle in the middle of a paved street near the waterfront. A plaque on the wall of a tavern on the corner was all that identified the site where Crispus Attucks had fallen along with Gray, Maverick, Carr, and Caldwell almost two hundred years before.

The buses unloaded. People on the street passed by without a glance. It didn't seem to strike anyone as strange to see loads of black people making their way from the buses to the cobblestone circle, devotees jockeying for position, pulling their collars up against the bitter winds blowing in from the bay. We stood at the outer rim of the group, holding a flag as the brief program began. There were a few speeches, a moment of silence, a curious feeling of turning inward during that moment. The cold wind numbed the mind and body and mercifully, the moment of silence ended. The homage was over as quickly as it began. People moved silently back onto the buses for the ride back to the hotel and the next event in their lives.

The flight back was brief; we didn't have enough time to dissect the messages we had been given by the power group the night before. We knew they were not pleased that we had come to Boston, but it was difficult to fathom the real source of the displeasure. Was the concept of the flag distasteful and repugnant to discuss? Was it that we had on financial package to offer and no foreseeable profit to be shared? Was it that we had secured endorsement from Thomas and the Boston Society without their having consulted with the rest of the leadership? Was it that they knew that the flag was being unfurled in Newark that very day?

Gleason and I realized no answer. Speculation was our only out. Speculation went down the drain more quickly than we thought possible. We left the plane. The only real question that absorbed us was the critical one: Is the flag flying?

We had packed brochures and a very large flag carefully for deposit at the Newark City Hall before we left for Boston. As we packed we had joked about "little Linden" being put to shame by "nervous Newark." When we had had enough laughter, we talked quietly about whether a few months had made the critical difference between rejection and acceptance. Then we wondered just how important it had been to city fathers that the request had the support of an established organization and whether fear of what might happen if the request were denied had played a part in their decision to unfurl the flag in Newark. We shrugged off the questions before too long and moved on to get ready to go to Boston secure in the knowledge that, at long last, the flag would fly at a seat of government in a major city.

It was not until we got off the plane in Newark that we began to worry that somehow, something had gone wrong, that the flag would not be in place, that maybe the group we had talked with the night before would have sabotaged the effort, that we wouldn't see the flag on the pole.

The drive from the airport to City Hall was too long! From twelve blocks away we craned our necks as we neared Broad Street hoping that we could see it, if it were there. Impossible! The next best thing was not to look. We'd just drive there, park nonchalantly, and then turn our eyes upward.

It was there!

We got out of the car, went up the steps and stood there on that cold afternoon, looking at the flag take the wind and move freely with it. We were warmed by the sight; a deep feeling of pride, success and plain joy at seeing the flag turn and flap in the windy day made us speechless. Gleason stood so still it was impossible to know that he was almost in pain from the relief of seeing it there. He felt, as I, that the day was a crowning point for all our efforts. We were looking at the flag atop a pole in a major city, recognized and acknowledged for what it represented.

Chapter 4

Images of the flag atop that pole flooded my dream that night, wiping away the unpleasant, memories of the put-down we had been given in Boston. Sleep was fitful, my excitement so great at seeing the flag I could hardly wait for the next day and another reassuring look at City Hall. We made it our business to contact friends there to get some inside reactions to the unfurling. Those reactions were mixed.

We were told that City Hall employees came to the windows to see for themselves and to smile with pride at knowing that the flag was there. The same evening, there were visitors to the Mayor's Office demanding to know what had given him the right to put up any "black" flag. These people indicated that they would "let the Mayor know when there was a flag to put up," and until then he wasn't to do anything without their say-so. We felt these people shared the philosophy that a flag should fly only if it had planes and guns and ships and airplanes behind it. They wanted the red, white, and blue as a standard because it had all those necessary armaments of war and defense to support it. Their concern was less with their pride than with their hides. They were concerned, too, with just how the white folks in the community would react to the flag.

Perhaps these were the people in the late '60s whose personal philosophies led them to say, "I'm not black; I am Negro and you'd better not call me black. I had to fight to be called a Negro." Perhaps their overriding concern for the defense of self that was implied somehow in the Stars and

Stripes of their grave worries about how the white community would react were of more importance to them than any opportunity to see this symbol given a place of honor on that one day. In any event, the belated word we received of these negative responses did not deter us in any way from the course we had charted.

The next major event on our agenda was participation in the Crispus Attucks Parade in late March, again in Newark.

We had decided to seek permission to participate in that parade with a contingent from Elizabeth. The group was composed of sixty-five young black people who almost, but not quite, fit the general description of "community-activists." Like many such black community groups which sprang up in cities across the country as blacks began to think through their needs, go to seats of power, and express the wishes of their communities, this group was vocal, but thoughtful. It was a new breed of organized young black people, bound together by a purpose to make things better somehow, but lacking the solidity and the stolidity of the old established black organizations like the NAACP and the Urban League. They did not form around a major charismatic figure. The group was simply a coming together of concerned, vocal, young blacks whose awareness of the complexities of the civil rights struggle was just beginning to emerge and to engage their thoughtful attention. The members of the group were impatient for change but did not urge a violent approach to effect that change.

Gleason and I joined them shortly after the group was formed and not long after the first publicity about the flag. It almost seemed that a special confluence of action resulted from our work with them. Endorsement of the flag was one of their earliest actions. Their eagerness to march in the parade was one more manifestation of the need for black pride that impelled them to meet weekly and to sit on the edge of their seats as they heard speakers bring a point of view. Marching in a parade carrying small flags appeared to be a healthy presentation of their point of view. All sixty-five agreed to march the quarter-mile from Symphony Hall to Military Park in the blistering cold March weather.

We did not have enough flags for each member of the group to carry one. Our funds had not allowed us to purchase the sixty-five flags. We wound up with twenty-one small banners on seven foot birchwood poles for the contingent. There were no uniforms, only enthusiasm.

We had asked the group to meet us at Lincoln Park prior to parade time. They were all there, dressed warmly against the weather and excited about the opportunity to be in the parade. We formed seven rows of five abreast with the man or woman at the ends of the rows carrying a small flag. I led the group with a mint flag on a ten-foot pole. At step-off time, we were together! It was a short march that seemed to last a long time; it was a moment to be savored as we marched along hearing people say, "There's the flag!" Recognition had come again.

As we passed giving an eyes-right, my eyes caught those of the woman who had objected so strenuously to the flag up in Boston. Puffed up in displeasure she stood there, in her mink coat . Her eyes blazed with anger. The intensity of that anger dissipated for me as we passed the stand and heard the crowd's applause. A little further down the street I saw Gleason standing with his wife and daughter and my family on the edge of the sidewalk. He smiled broadly as we passed. For a moment I wondered why he had chosen not to march, leaving the contingent just after it had formed but that was a passing thought. Gleason was not one for center stage. His retiring manner permeated his actions and rarely did he make a decision that put him out front. He usually stood quietly on the side when we made speaking appearances, leaving the presentations to me. It would have been uncharacteristic of him had he chosen to march.

When the parade ended, we were all tired yet invigorated. It had been an extraordinary moment for us. This was the first time the flag had been on display in a parade. It had come a long way.

The flag had been displayed at other times and in other ways that brought us great concern. In November 1967, a school disturbance erupted in Linden. "Racial unrest," as the media called it, had developed into a protest march by black students led by a young man carrying the flag. As students neared the steps of the school, they were met by policemen blocking their approach. The next day, reporters headlined stories and pictures with the words: Demonstrators Use Black Nationalist Flag. When these headlines appeared, we talked with reporters about what we called a misprint. Our insistence that the flag was not a nationalist flag was met with casual comments: "What's the difference?" There was a difference; the flag had been put in the wrong context and we wanted clarification, a follow-up statement indicating the error. We didn't get it. The newspapers were only willing to give us the assurance that "liberation" and "Nationalist" would not be attached to future reference of the flag.

Somewhere along the line a reporter had said to us that violence would put the flag front center. He had said bluntly, "Blood picks up ink." He had certainly been right where the incident with the students in Linden had been concerned. The flag got more attention than the cause the students had placed behind it. That negative attention was not what we sought. The whole incident made us realize how fragile was our hold on how and when the flag would come to public attention.

It seemed so urgent from this experience to be as certain as possible that the public was made to understand what the flag represented. If it were to be displayed, at least the displayer should have a sense of what it was about. Perhaps that incident in Linden solidified more than anything else the content of the talks we gave. We had a most compelling need to drive home its meaning, its reason for existence. The flag was not intended to be a rallying point for a particular group or interest within the black race. Wherever we went after that incident we offered it as a standard banner to serve as a common denominator with which all blacks could identify and not as the particular property of a special interest group within our people.

We took the message wherever we could. The Black Students Organization of Howard University invited us to make a presentation there. We took the train to Washington carrying only a couple of boxes of decals and a flag. Gleason's sister-in-law, a student at Howard, met us at the station brimming of plans to show us the campus and get us to the auditorium filled with students and professors. This was one of our earliest appearances at a college campus. It established our expectations of student response to the flag that were fulfilled whatever campus we visited.

Gleason and I both spoke that afternoon. The students were genuinely and enthusiastically interested in the flag. Their questions focused on the design process, how we moved it to the public, what they might do to spread the word even more, and whether we had flags they could purchase. We had no flags for sale; we did have the decals which we distributed to them. Borrowing from our experience at the high school in Linden, we emphasized the importance of the appropriate display of the banner and decals. This audience gave every indication that they did indeed understand the symbolism we intended to under gird the flag and would keep the philosophical meanings we had discussed.

We didn't know it then, but in only a few months we would try to collect on their promises--with some unexpected results.

The appearance at Howard University was good for us. During the next several months we spoke at many campuses. Black college students were always exciting audiences; their fervor about equality and the struggle to acquire it was almost unmatched by any other segment of the black community. Middle class students were particularly insistent on achieving the recognition that the flag was intended to symbolize. They, and elderly black men and women, were probably the most responsive of all audiences we met. The young had nothing to lose by voicing their needs to have their fundamental rights accorded to them; they stood to gain a more decent and fulfilling future than their parents had experiences. The older black man and woman had nothing to lose either; they stood to gain the self respect that was the satisfying feeling they could take to the grave with them. Pride in self could warm old bones faster than any heavenly robe and golden slippers. Voicing their pleasure about the flag was one way of articulating their connection to distant Africa. Those old people always told us, "You boys are doing a good thing. Keep it up." Their encouragement and that of the young people we encountered kept us moving on a full schedule.

In April 1968, the Fourth Ward Political Club held its annual breakfast, a local activity that was usually well-supported by the community. We were asked to provide a flag for display at the breakfast. Inadvertently someone let slip that we were going to be the honorees. We were pleased by this gesture even though it was difficult to pretend that we were unaware of what was coming. We arrived that morning with the flag and found a large audience including the mayor and our ward councilman. After all the speeches, an announcement was made that the organization was presenting its "Man of the Year" award to two men. Our names were called; we were given plaques and the hall filled with applause.

Gleason spoke first, his quiet words impressing the audience. The man's complete commitment to the flag overrode his shyness and touched people as he spoke of what the flag meant to him and how deeply he appreciated the honor given to it and to him. When it came my turn, the only thought that crossed my mind rose from a long-buried memory of being ignored in school when awards were given to students. I had been told once, by the principal of my high school, that the reason I never received any awards was because he had never known me to raise any hell in the school so he didn't know me. The words came easily as I told the Fourth Ward Political Club about that memory and that the only reason I was receiving an award in Linden was because a little hell had been raised. The audience broke out in laughter, everyone joining in except the white councilman who represented our ward. He stared at me as though he was trying to figure out where in hell I had come from. The black residents of the ward understood what I meant. Recognition seldom came to black students, black residents or black citizens from any source other than themselves.

It felt good to be honored by neighbors. It was a high point for each of us and we spent the rest of the afternoon talking quietly at my house about the experiences we had had and the little successes we felt we had achieved. This recognition was something special; we were grateful for it.

The exhilaration of the honor carried over into the next day at work. My hands flew through the pieces of a display under construction and things fell into place easily. Gleason and I met as usual at lunch time to talk about appointments we had scheduled for appearances. Our conversation returned time and again to the good feelings we had as a result of the honor received the day before. The euphoria lingered hours later when the work day was over.

After dinner that night I went into the TV room, turned on the set and eased into a chair with the plaque in my hand. I remember sitting there enjoying the feel of the engraved plate on the wooden base of the plaque when a bulletin interrupted the newscast. Martin Luther King had been shot!

The plaque suddenly weighed a ton in my hand. I let it slide onto the chair and sat there in disbelief at what I was hearing and beginning to see unfold on the set in front of me.

Some madman somewhere in Memphis had just turned life into death, victory into ashes, joy into a tearing, shredding pain.

Martin Luther King was dead! The peace and non-violence he had espoused were about to become angry, violent, rampaging forces unleashed on the streets of American cities. But for now, it was a time of raw feeling, a sense of having been tortured and flayed. It was a time when the body refused to move, when taking a breath was agony. It was a time to hold on to some small voice coming from the deeper recesses of the mind singing, "We Shall Overcome," a plaintive, bittersweet sound telling of hope and belief in right and expectation of justice. Martin Luther King had lived a life of selflessness in his pursuit of higher ideals. He had made things possible for the black man that some had never dreamed could ever be-- little things, like being able to sit anywhere on a bus, like going into a voting booth and casting a ballot for the first time without the intimidation of having to recite verbatim a whole section of the Constitution before you could even register to vote. Little things! Things he made possible by pricking the conscience of white America and shoving some steel into the backbone of the Constitution. He had walked with garbage men and talked with kings, paid some heavy dues in jail, endured the thousand eyes that watched every move he made, and still lived out his commitment to a dream that America could fulfill its promise even to the black man. He had talked, to those of us who would listen, about peace. Peace and nonviolence, change and the coming of a new order for this society. He was, for a time, the drum major for a movement that had not even acknowledged its own existence, a movement recoiling from the horrors and injustices of a morally wrong and senseless war.

The television set brought him into that room that night. He was saying that he might not get to the "Promised Land" but he had been to the mountaintop and looked over at it. His face seemed etched with pain. Perhaps it was the pain of his vision, his sense of never being able to do all that he wanted to do, that made his face seem different somehow as it appeared on the screen. I know that those last public words were a particular moment of grandeur for him. The words summed up for me what he had sought to accomplish and they were not self-aggrandizing words spoken to achieve fame or fortune or applause. He had set out to do something for his fellow man; he had demonstrated a willingness to deny self in the process. He had indeed seen the promised land and earned a place there. He laid down the burden he had carried, the burden of awakening a collective consciousness, laid it down in pain, receiving a bitter peace in return.

I could not watch television in the days that followed. I had no desire to see the funeral and march or hear the words or see the faces of the nation. The funeral was of no meaning to me. He had been what was real.

Legislation flowed like the River Jordan in the wake of King's death. Doors opened that had been nailed shut, the nails melted by the fires in the streets. Black people held meetings and marched. White people held their mea culpa sessions. Still the divisions between peoples grew; still the most terrible fires flamed--the fires of hatred, revulsion and bitterness that drove a heated wedge between the people of this country. The peace he had sought, the nonviolence he had advocated seemed to be more elusive and impossible to achieve than before.

It seemed no time to talk of pride when anger was the black man's uppermost emotion, yet we were asked to come before more and more audiences in the weeks after King's assassination. We exhausted ourselves before clubs, at churches, on college campuses, at community gatherings. Our message remained the same: the flag is a symbol of pride in a people whose roots go back to the earliest of times on a continent that gave birth to a rich heritage of arts, music, the humanities. The flag was a symbol of endurance, contribution, heritage, and recognition of that from which we had come. The flag told of what we wanted in and for the future.

That was the message.

We believed it was heard. College students ran up the flag on their campuses in the weeks after King's death and kept it there at half-mast. And there were stirrings of even more positive efforts underway in the country as the Poor People's March on Washington came nearer to its scheduled day.

We seemed to have become a people accustomed to making our statements in the streets. If only a few could tread hallowed halls, whether on campus or in Congress, many could find a piece of pavement on which to plant their feet and take a stand. The Poor People's March was going to memorialize King while the problems of the poor were articulated once more.

Gleason and I talked about the possibility of our going to Washington for at least one day of the "march" and began to explore ways to make contacts with the Campaign managers to determine what we needed to do to make a little room for the flag.

We approached the Poor People's Campaign managers as the well publicized showpiece mules struck off from points South headed toward Resurrection City. We wanted permission to have the flag unfurled at the site and to distribute decals at a nominal price, a few pennies above cost. John went to Washington to make the inquiry for us. He took with him our offer to make a contribution to the campaign from the small profit derived from the sale of decals. We sent a complete package of information about the flag, copies of news articles and brochures, and relied on John to convey verbally a sense of what we were trying to do with the flag. As he left we ordered decals and small flags and renewed our contacts with students at Howard University hoping that they would meet with us on the critical day of the march, June 19, and help distribute the decals.

John was able to make contact with middle level organizers of the Campaign and to them he laid out our wishes and requests. He received a non-negotiable response that a flat fifty percent of all monies derived from the sale of decals had to go into the Campaign coffers. When he returned with this news, we realized that to meet this stipulation and cover the cost of the printing we would have to increase the sale price to twice what we had planned.

The decals would be exorbitantly priced and we would appear to be gougers!

We agonized over this prospect. It was difficult to reconcile our desire to be there, flag and decals in hand, with the demands of the organizers for monies that would be out of reach if a fair sale price were put on the decals. We weighed the disadvantages of going to Washington as just another side-walk huckster-without-credentials versus the near impossible accredited sale at outrageous prices. We sat down and looked at the boxes of decals. There were 50,000 little slips in the boxes; they were bright, colorful, the words "Black is Beautiful" in bold letters on the right hand side, a replica of the flag on the left, all against a florescent yellow background. We thought about the thousands of people who would be in Washington, about the pos-sibility of reaching out to some of them, talking with them about the flag, making them aware of what it could mean to us as a people. The possibility was too enormous to ignore. We had to make the hard decision to go with the approval or go on our own and take our chances.

We chose to not make the deal with the Campaign staff. We chose to go with what we had and hope that things would work out in a way that was not demeaning to the flag.

As the Campaign took shape, amorphous as it was, we wondered how the flag or our presentation of it in any form could hinder the Campaign from reaching its goals. The media gleefully announced the self-fulfilling prophecies of violence about to be spawned in Washington and reported in detail the lack of organization that appeared evident among the clamoring leaders of the Campaign. The menu of demands presented by Ralph Aber-nathy on behalf of the poor and dispossessed was scanned daily for signs of unpalatability. When Bayard Rustin was called in to salvage the planning of the March, some papers took a more compassionate stand while others raked over the instances of mismanaged marches that had occurred under his leadership and that of others. There seemed to be a few who understood that the Campaign and the apex of its thrust, the march, was important to the thousands of people who would somehow get to Washington to present themselves as visible evidence of the poverty that could no longer be dis-missed from thought in this country.

Washington had seen marches before. Veterans, women, the handicapped, environmentalists, beekeepers; everybody with a cause had descended on the city at one time or another. This time, again this time, it was the poor, the undereducated, the underemployed, the neglected, the oppressed.

They were arriving in huge numbers; the forecasts had been fairly accurate in terms of anticipated attendance and were bolstered by the large numbers of people who planned to attend as a personal statement about Martin Luther King, Jr.

We got ready to go knowing in advance that altruism and hunger were not the incentives for some who would be among the thousands-hunger of the stomach, that is. There were those heading there who hungered for power, money, media exposure, quick adventure, and impersonal encounters with faceless and nameless bodies. A gathering such as this was ideal for meeting those needs; there were those who meant to take advantage of the opportunity.

We wanted to publicize the flag. Maybe that made us opportunists too, just like those who hungered for the media exposure that their speeches would get for them. We just could not let a chance pass us by to take what we felt was a fitting symbol of black people's aspirations to those who were gathering in the capitol.

On the afternoon of June 18th we loaded my car with the many boxes of decals. As often happened with us, getting on the road meant some comic relief. My car was so overloaded the rear end snagged everything in sight on the road. We arrived in Washington with a sigh of relief and a pat for the front end of the car. It had gotten us there!

We drove first to Howard University, looking for the students who had promised to help us "in any way possible." We found most of them taking mid-term examinations in their summer session classes and we knew that we would not try to take them away from that. There were a few who could help and we had the car unloaded in short order. After locating a small motel on the outskirts of Washington where we could stay for the night, we returned to the campus, reloaded the car and headed for the center of Resurrection City on the mall. Some students accompanied us and helped unload the car. We gave each one a few boxes of decals, established a time for reporting back to us and let them go to the crowds milling on the great space between the monuments. We had asked them to spend a few minutes talking about the flag and its purpose before they offered the decals for sale. In a way each student became an emissary for the flag as we relied on the personal communication skills of these young people to reach as many as possible of the thousands gathered on the mall.

Gleason and I set up a small stand at the fringe of the main body of the crowd and stood in the sweltering heat of the muggy afternoon and evening talking with people about the flag and selling decals as requests were made. The students reported back to us as the evening ended, bringing unsold decals and full accounts of monies from sales along with their impressions of people's interest in the flag. The young people seemed eager to return the next morning and give us a hand as they had promised.

The next day, the day of the long march, the city seemed to wake especially early in readiness for the event. We encountered a massive amount of traffic as we made our way back to the site and gathered the students around our small stand.We knew Bayard Rustin had been replaced after the internecine wranglings among the organizers and we wondered , whether things would go well. We hoped that it would be a successful day, a positive presentation of the needs of Americas poor.

We looked at the crowds and listened to the speeches which blew across the mall, creating the only breezes that day. We missed the presence and voice of Martin Luther King, an absense made more painful by the frequent refrences to him. We listened too, as comments rippled through the crowds about how Ralph Abernathy had been forced to reconsider his choice of resting place at night and had made the decision to move to the Campaign site, abandoning the comfort of the motel headquarters he had established. The people had acknowledged his move, making him "Mayor" of Resurrection City, and they were proud of him for coming around.

The camp site was important to the people; it was essential to experience it first-hand in order to feel part of the whole campaign. As we stood in the sun we heard others talk about their sense of what made the campsite a desirable place to be; these men snapped their suspender straps as they described the "action," white action to be found in some of the tents pitched as far as you could see along the mall.

As the day moved along, we took on a contact high from the sweet aromas of marijuana that meshed with the musk of the sweating crowds. We saw the litter pile up on the face of the city.

We tried to talk to everyone who passed our stand, condensing our usual speeches to the fewest possible words to grab attention and interest. We finally folded our table and packed it in. The day had been long and we had done the best we could do in the heat and noise of the shifting crowds. The students reported back to us once more. We thanked them for their efforts and wished them well in their pursuit of education. We hoped that if they would focus on acquiring every bit of learning they could, they might avoid the horrors of life experienced by the thousands of people who had come to Washington almost literally on the last pennies they had.

We packed our boxes and left the city, too tired at first to do much talking. As we drove through Maryland, Delaware, and onto the New Jersey Turnpike, we began to revive as cars passed us, cars heading north with decals plastered on their bumpers. We were returning with boxes of decals, thousands of them; we had barely met expenses. Yet we were seeing the message of the decals traveling to other parts of the country on the cars which passed and that was what was important.

Our conversation picked up, focusing again and again on our impressions of the march and the feelings of disappointment we each had. We worried aloud whether there would be any productive or positive movement, whether America could rise to the challenge of meeting the needs of her poor, whether indeed we MUST always have the poor among us -- a balancing weight to the prosperity enjoyed by others. We wondered whether black leaders could generate within themselves the kind of sophisticated altruism and purpose we thought essential to achieve a measure of upper mobility for all our people. The cant of the church had moved the emotions of the black people gathered on the mall, but did little to stimulate the white majority on the other side of the TV screens replaying the scene. We needed speeches that played to the pockets of the philanthropists, it was true. But someone needed to make black people see that the resources we had among ourselves could be pooled to become working capital for the development of banks and small industries, economic institutions that could provide jobs and mortgage money and more capital for more economic growth. The March on Washington had been a plea for handouts. We needed to learn to use our resources to help ourselves and leave handouts to those who were truly helpless. Black people had more resources than our spiritual power and the March had not tapped it.

Chapter 5

The Poor People's Campaign taught us that we were sheer novices at marketing an idea. We did not know how to go about developing or implementing a grand strategy that would effectively plant the flag forefront in the consciousness of our people any more than the March leaders had had a real strategy for utilizing the resources of Black America. We could return only to the thing we did best at that time; we continued to make speeches and appearances wherever we were asked.

College campuses were still a major center for discussion and dissemination of the concept of the flag. We received invitations over the summer months to visit campuses and these intensified when the fall semester began. We went to Rutgers University, Baruch College, New York University and City College of New York, to speak to Black student organizations. Student interest had always been high, but there seemed to be a new quality to the questions they were asking and the thoughts they were expressing as we talked with them about the flag. "Black power" was becoming more than a raised fist. Students seemed to be asking for a new sense of direction from the older generation of Black Americans. They wanted assurance that there was a good future in store for them, that opportunities to prove their value in the marketplace were going to be available, that their faith in the goodness of being what they were - black people - was going to be recognized and valued by the power structure they so clearly defined and identified.

Their enthusiasm was infectious. They bought flags to hang beside their fraternity and sorority insignias in the dormitories and wanted to hear what it represented, wanted to internalize those symbols. They seemed to reach for the full symbolism as though the flag could give them the rallying point from which they would make an assault on the world waiting outside for them. They were eager and proud of their enthusiasm.

Not everyone was enthusiastic or eager to be associated with us or the flag. We found that backstabbing was a reality when you took a deep breath and went out to the world with something you believed to be a natural and desirable idea. Some friends became former acquaintances. That was the easy way out of being too closely associated with us. Others were more outspoken, advising us that they perceived "political ramifications" where the flag was concerned. We agreed with them. There were ramifications; they appeared if one did nothing else but hang the flag on a pole outside the house. Each of us had installed a pole out front soon after the first newspaper article appeared. And soon after we placed the flags outside, police patrols doubled in our neighborhood. "Ramifications" for us, meant suspected tapping into our telephone; a peculiar echo in the connection seeming to signal some surveillance we did not welcome. We did not fear being watched; there was nothing to hide. The media had covered fairly the intent and content of the flag in the first articles. The brochures were strong in content, but spoke our minds for us as plainly as we could say it. We endured the chill in the atmosphere at our respective jobs. We persevered in our pursuit of promoting attention to the flag at personal expense. We knew well what "ramifications" meant.

It was difficult to understand, and harder to accept, attitudes among those in the black community who seemed to take a " we'll wait and see" posture. It seemed to be marked with the unspoken words "wait and see what the white man thinks about it" - before minds could be made up to applaud, recognize, accept, or endorse the flag as a concept or as a reality. Those who wanted to wait and see would not buy decals or display a flag. Instead, their cars sported decals which featured a "tiger in the tank". They spoke disparagingly of "pride." "What do we have to be proud of in a society where we are dispossessed, ignored, tortured in the spirit if not the flesh?", they seemed to ask as though they had heaped these degradations upon themselves.

Others whispered behind our backs that they thought we were trying to rip off the community through the sale of flags and decals. And still others in a way that told us they meant to ignore us and if ignored long enough we would somehow go away and leave them in their comfortable positions of dictating and articulating the thinking of black people.

Maybe some were jealous of our development of the concept. It was hard to pin that down, but the current of emotions began to run strongly in our town as we continued to keep our commitments to speak and present the flag over June and July of 1968. Sometimes our best indicator of where the nay-sayers lurked was in the absence of an invitation to appear before a community group.

We tried not to take it personally, not to feel that we were somehow wrong to want to promote a concept of pride, as we spent long evenings in assessing where we had been and where we seemed to be going as the summer months waned. And we tried to spend more time with our families for a change. Our daughters were growing and developing, our homes needed more attention than we had been giving. Gleason and his wife had discovered that a second baby was on the way. It was time to take a breather.

It was now nearly a year and a half since that Sunday Gleason had spoken about a flag in his living room. We had been many places in that time, met hundreds of people, received and read thousands of letters, ploughed our personal resources into the effort, met with some successes in developing awareness of the flag. Still, we knew, we had made only a small dent in the conscious awareness within people.

The summer hiatus soon ended; it was time to return to our preoccupation. August would see the Third Black Power Conference meeting in Philadelphia and we planned to be there with the flag. We hoped that we might find some answers to our questions about how to stretch our time and resources to pay off more fully in broadening awareness of the flag.

We arranged time off from our jobs for the three days we would spend in Philadelphia. This time we did not seek advance approval for attending the Conference. We sent no brochures, asked no endorsements; we just went.

That summer had seen the continuing focus of attention on the plight, anger, frustrations, and hopes of black people voiced through the designated leadership of the traditional and "new" black organizations. The leadership was probably at its crest of media exposure in articulating the wants and needs of blacks. Anybody who could claim a membership or a following got his time on television and attention to his applications for grants. The Black Power Conference was going to try once again to weld together a united force for action. Barring that, it would create another forum for the voicing of the many opinions and agendas that would be brought to Philadelphia.

We prepared for the trip, boxing a few small flags and decals, and filling cartons with new handouts we felt explained our point of view about the flag and events as we saw them occurring in the '60s. We loaded into Gleason's car this time, knowing that he had problems with the driver's seat in the '59 model, but it was, after all, his turn to drive.

The New Jersey Turnpike can be a rather monotonous road to travel. We filled the time with our usual musings about the possible reception we might get and speculating whether the new handouts we were taking would grab the attention of those attending the conference. We were dependent on the literature and the visual impact of the flag to make a point for us. Or conversation turned to the content of the handouts and in particular to the plea to force some recognition of people and events in Black American history that we felt deserved commemoration. The list was not original with us; we were adding our voices to those heard in many civil rights meetings, voices asking for acknowledgment of the work of Medger Evers and Martin Luther King Jr., Memorializing of the four little girls who had died in the bombing of the church in Birmingham, recognition of Malcom X, Paul Robeson, Crispus Attucks, and even the anniversary of the arrival of the first slave in America. There were so many black people whose lives had been played out in stark and tragic moments in American history whose names and contributions were not given any recognition. The Booker T. Washington - George Washington Carver kind of recognition tucked away in center pages of books gave our children so little to hang their hats on as they studied American history. If there were ever going to be any purposeful strengthening of awareness of the contributions of black people to the growth and development of this country, we would have to ask for it. We were asking in the handout for this kind of recognition and pleading to our people to come together in a concerted way to demand some commemoration of important people and events.

Once again, we were heading to a gathering of the more powerful of black leadership and hoping as we went that something positive would emerge from these few days. The conference was held in a church in Center City. We hadn't made advance reservations and couldn't get into any hotel near the conference site. We decided to try to find accommodations farther out but first we found a man at the church to stand watch over the boxes we wanted to unload there. He charged us a small fee for the service and promised we'd find him and the boxes there when we returned.

We started off to look for a hotel. Gleason was tired so I took over the wheel. As well as I knew Gleason I just didn't know his car. We had no more than started down Broad Street when the seat gave way under me and I found myself lying on the floor, my eyes barely above window level. A woman in the car next to us took one look and took off as fast as she could. We pulled over, jacked up the seat with a cinder block we found on the curb, and kept looking for a place to stay. We found a hotel about four miles away, unloaded our bags and turned around immediately to go back to the conference site.

As soon as we arrived the man looking out for our boxes told us, that people had expressed an interest in the literature and the flag. They wanted to buy; we had very little to sell. We set up a table on the sidewalk outside the church, laid out what we had, and passed out the literature as fast as we could. We saw Ron Karenga, Nathan Wright, Floyd McKissick, and Amiri Baraka stride purposefully into the church within the space of a few minutes. Others of note passed as we stood on the hot pavement watching and wishing we had some way to appeal to them for a few minutes talk about the flag.

We were overwhelmed by the positive statements we heard from people as they passed the table, read the handout and looked at the small banner on display. None of the power-brokers stopped. We lasted in the heat for about three hours, responding to queries about the flag. We made appointments to talk in more detail with groups of delegates at our hotel that evening.

We grabbed dinner and went looking for a state store to buy some wine to provide a few throat quenchers for those who had promised to stop by the room. People arrived in little groups throughout the evening; conversation slackened only long enough for introductions to be made. Their questions made us realize that they sensed value in the concept of the flag. They wanted to know when and how the idea was developed, what had been the reaction of the community - white and black - whether we had tried to market through a company or considered mass production as a cottage industry. They asked, ASKED, permission to march with the flag back in their home towns.

Nobody drank the wine; the bottles were still capped and full when the last person left. This had been one of the best and most serious discussions we had had with anyone about true promotion of the concept.

Most gratifying was that not one person suggested possible profit; instead, they focused on the need to raise the level of awareness and consciousness of the flag. They gave us food for thought and we were pleased to have our thinking stimulated by questions and suggestions.

The next morning we heard a radio newscast. The Black Power Conference was being described and, to our surprise, the newscaster was talking about the "Black Flag." The voice described it in detail, probably using a copy of the handout, and gave our names. We were almost knocked off our feet; this was exposure we had not expected. We threw on our dashikis, true to the times, and headed out without breakfast to get back to the church.

It was minor bedlam around our table that morning. People insisted on buying the decals and the small stock of flags we had with us. By the middle of the afternoon we had completely sold the banners and just about exhausted the supply of handouts. We decided to sit in on sessions, taking turns at the table outside.

As in Newark the year before, it was a multi-hued group of people. The many variations in skin color confirmed the extent to which the African in us had been diluted but also confirmed that blackness was not a color. The variations in speech, from the slow drawl of the Southerners to the faster speech of Northern delegates, told of the consuming interest of black people throughout the country in effecting social change. The multitude of patterns in the dashikis, worn by virtually every man, were eye-catching. What was more exciting was the umpteen kinds of handshakes that were going around. It was impossible to get the full impact of those variations until you tried to respond to one - from fingers to palm, to arm, and back to fingers again. Some of the more exotic of those greeting rituals seemed to take five minutes.

We saw all of this. We talked to as many people as we could that day. Some promised to ask the conference to endorse the flag in the final sessions on Sunday morning. When the resolution was offered that morning, the conference leaders announced that it would be brought up at the next conference and that was that. It had been worth it; we were glad we had gone.

Christmas '68 passed and we entered the New Year, knowing that we would have to do some serious thinking about how we could best promote awareness of the flag. Things slowed down for us as Gleason and his wife became parents for the second time. It was a beautiful baby girl and he took special delight in holding her for long stretches of time.

He would remark, as he held her, that our children have always seemed to hold out a special hope. He was right; we somehow believed that if things were not going to be better for adults, the next generation would harvest a crop of happiness and success. That baby, we hoped, would see the flag accepted by black people and flown as a symbol of hope and pride.

He wanted to spend more time with his family so we slowed down on accepting the invitations that came to us and held ourselves to no more than two engagements a week. By early April, we were knuckling down to the difficult process of developing a real strategy for broadcasting news of the flag.

We had no real insight into how to do that. We had no power base from which to secure an endorsement that would carry to the farthest reaches of all black communities. We had no money resources to initiate even the cottage industry approach mentioned in Philadelphia, despite its appeal. We had no idea how to market the product even if we had resources to produce it. We were exhausting our personal resources for travel, no matter how short the distance. Printers were willing to let us defer payment as we ordered new brochures, but a debt is a debt and must be paid. It was cash on the line whenever we ordered additional flags. Postage was an ogre eating at our pockets.

We spent many evenings that early spring of '69 talking about possible ways to draw national attention. None of those ways seemed within reach. We did interest people in the face-to-face meetings we had at our many appearances, it was true. It appeared that word of mouth, was our only way to keep viable the concept of the flag. We would just have to keep relying on that until the hoped for opportunity would present itself.

Part of our problem in focusing that spring on feasible means to promote the flag was the fact that we were each going through personal changes. Gleason was unhappy at the chemical plant, and I, sensing the fast growing hostility at my job, had already made steps to change employers. Gleason talked about opening a small bakery in the community. He enjoyed the thought that something he could do well could also be a source of income. He worried that his energy would have to be diverted to the business and away from our speeches and meetings. It caused him real agony to consider what his withdrawal from visible and active promotion of the flag would mean in the eyes of the community. He also worried that opening his own business might fuel fires tended by those who thought we had made a financial killing from the flag. Those people would never believe that to open his own place he would have to go out on a limb, willing to mortgage everything.

I knew that he wanted both things to succeed -- his business and our cause. Somehow we could still pursue this quest. We let the pace slow a little more as he began to turn his thoughts to getting a business off the ground. The spring blossomed around us as we spent a little more time at our homes and with our families. He stopped by my house on Memorial Day with April. They were on the way to visit his parents and he had happened to see me working outside in the yard. We talked about the latest Mets game, his baby's rapid growth, and the best way to fight the crabgrass in my lawn. He didn't stay long, promising that we would meet the following Thursday. Something came up though, and he didn't make it to my house that evening.

Nine days later he was dead, in an accident at the plant he had wanted so much to leave.

Chapter 6

Breezes from the ocean lifted tendrils of black dried seaweed and moved them gently to new resting places on the buff sand. The bank rose sharply to where the sand was warm, alive with little creatures darting among the shells some child had heaped in an afternoon of play on the beach. Perhaps the shells had been part of a "hanger" for spacecraft, larger in the child's mind than any adult could conceive in reality, the hanger a shelter for the spaceships that moved in erratic dartings from the tiny triangular openings of the shell structure. Creatures still moved out from the ruins of the shells, searching the cosmos of that sand for the riches it held.

There was little to hamper their movement on the beach. A lone fisherman waded now and then into the surf to stand knee deep in the grey-brown water, white caps licking at his boots. He thrust his hat back to glance up at the cloudy sky then down the shoreline to where grey skies and sand commingled. When the sun broke through, he pulled his hat down and, hands on hips, watched the water glide and rush in toward him, making the sands shift beneath his feet. He stood there for a long time until the line from the pole planted behind him went taut and he turned to tend to his reason for being there.

Terns and gulls played their aerial games, ignoring me and the fisherman. Every now and then one dropped out to rest on the scraggly fencing that leaned over to mark the line of vegetation inland on the island. When a team member cried out from the sky, the bird rose to rejoin the formation, finding his prescribed position with ease and certainty.

The fisherman left, catch box loaded with one fish, the time for solitude ended.

The beach was deserted now. Except for the birds there was no one to bear witness to the tears I did not fight. It was so easy and so difficult to let them flow, the salty water from my eyes at home near the brine of the ocean.

I wept for my dead friend, for his youth, his children and wife, for a life that no longer was, and the dreams that he could never fulfill.

It could not be that Gleason was dead. It could not be though I had seen the casket draped with the two flags he had served. I had heard the ministers speak in measured voices the words of consolation that never console. The church had been crowded and my wife and I had found seats in the balcony. Directly in front, as we looked down, the bronze box held Gleason's body. A young tenor voice had pierced the murmurs of the sorrowing as the words filled the church---"Facing the rising sun of a new day begun, let us march on til victory is won."

The funeral service was mercifully brief. As we left the church and moved outside I heard friends offer quiet words, "I'm sorry, sorry." A few laid a hand on my shoulder as they spoke these inadequate words. I reached in my pocket and pulled a handful of the Black American Flag buttons we had just had made up. I gave them to those I could reach as we made our way to the car.

The drive to the cemetery seemed to take a very long time. The radio was on softly and I remember the voice of Jerry Butler singing "Only the strong survive." My wife, a neighbor who had gone with us, and I rode in silence at the end of a long cartage. As we entered the cemetery I could see the hearse gliding and turning through the narrow lane until it came to a stop. Seeing it stop made a jolt flow through my body. This was impossible. Gleason was going to be put into the ground and we would have to leave him in this place.

It could not be so.

It was still not possible though I had sat on this beach for five mornings in a row, seeking an answer in the ocean's roar, some sounds that would deny the reality of his death.

None came. Nothing eased my pain. The birds still circled in the sky; the water still kept its primordial rhythms. Gleason was gone.

Gleason's death was the most painful experience of my life. The suddenness and incomprehensibility of it tore me apart. There had been nothing in the day that had gone wrong, nothing to warn of the enormous shock that would come. My new job took me into New York City and I had returned home in a company car, music on the radio smoothly bringing me down from the day's hectic pace, warm sun shining brightly under a brilliant blue sky. Life seemed very good, in fact.

As I pulled into my driveway, Mrs. Robinson, my neighbor, called out to me in a peculiarly strangled, excited voice.

"Did you hear the news over the radio?"

"What news?"

"About Gleason."

"No, what about him? What happened?" I walked across the lawn toward her as she lowered her voice.

"There was an explosion where Gleason works. He got hurt. I think he died. He got killed!"

Her voice was so low now I could hardly hear her. She seemed almost apologetic as she told me someone had tried to rush him to the hospital.

I turned from her, wanting to get into my house, needing to call his wife Miriam to find out if he was hurt. The neighbor's words " died" and "killed" were surely just overblown tragic words neighbors sometimes rushed to speak. I pulled off my jacket, needing to free myself from its unnecessary warmth as I started up the walk to my house.

My wife stood at the door. I stopped and looked at her face and tried to read it through the screen.

"Did you hear anything?" I asked her, not wanting to know, not wanting her to confirm Mrs. Robinson's message.

"Gleason's dead".

I froze for an instant, then recoiled as the shock wave behind the words struck me. I must have moved back a few steps and found myself immobilized against the gas lamp on the lawn. I slid down the lamppost, still looking at her.

"I can't believe that."

"Yes, he died this afternoon."

I put my head down, finally giving into the words.

My daughter, with a friend of hers, was suddenly at my side. She put her hand on my shoulder and asked what was wrong. I shook my head and tried to look at her, but my glasses were full of tears and I couldn't see her.

"Go and play. I'll be alright."

She took her hand away slowly, then leaned her head on my shoulder for a moment and ran off with her friend.

I sensed the nearness of my neighbors and heard them offer aid to my wife as she lifted my arm to help me stand. We went into the house.

I fell onto the sofa, unable to move any more. For hours I lay there trying to absorb the meaning of the words my neighbors and my wife had spoken. When the cloud of perplexity would not lift, I went to his house.

Miriam, his wife, was in tears. We cried together.

I was able, finally, to look away from her and to see the room and feel his presence. Everything was as it had been - table, chairs, stereo, sofa, drapes at the window, his oil painting on the wall. This was his home; these were his belongings. It was not right that he was not here.

I couldn't say anything to Miriam. There were only the touch of a hand and my tears to let her know that the agony of this Calvary was as real for me as it was for her.

I left his house and went to his parent's home. Many people were gathered outside the house. Most knew of the ties that bound us together, and it was their handshakes, given in silence, that sealed that feeling of despair that came over me.

His parents and sister were sitting quietly. I spoke a few words to each and left.

For four days I could not sleep more than a few minutes at a time. It took all the will power I possessed to dress for the funeral. The anger I had tried to control surfaced as we left the cemetery and passed corners filled with the flotsam of life, lounging against walls of bars, hanging onto the support of lampposts that were their only pillars of strength in this life. Why should people who hang on corners live for years and he die at only 32?

It was too easy to scream at those loungers in silent anger. They probably weren't even aware of the great waste they had made of themselves. They surely could not know the terrible waste of a life that his death meant to me and to those who knew him well.

There weren't many who did know him well. He had been one of life's quiet ones, moving in the small circles he had chosen and defined for himself--the circles of family, church, and work, that were so important to him. He had been a complex man who wanted no part of even the ordinary strife that ordinary people usually encountered as they lived out their lives.

I never heard him speak disparagingly of anyone. Even when we met with disillusioning remarks by those who put us and the flag down, he found some gracious way to turn the other cheek and remind me that we had to move on to the next audience, the next meeting, the next chance to reach somebody with the flag.

He was sensitive. He could not understand the greed we found in those we asked to work with us and it hurt him deeply to discover that human nature could manifest itself in that crude way when we were presenting an idea that had implications for an entire group of people. I guess it was his deep idealism that prevented him from coming to terms directly with the realities we were facing as we tried to promote his concept and our development of it that the flag represented.

As the first weeks passed after his death, I tried to put him into perspective, tried to understand what had brought his life into a parallel path with mine, what had been the meaning and reason for his existence. I sank into a melancholy search for solitude to find the answers to the questions I couldn't even frame out loud.

I grieved for him.

Every day that it was possible I rose early and drove alone to the beaches of South Jersey. I searched for the most isolated spots and was angry when someone else had gotten there first. The best of times came when there was nothing there but the sand and the endless water to become the oracle from whom I could seek answers.

One morning the sun rose from the seam of sky and sea, rose with a great burst of color, edging it's way up in a huge red-gold circle. I felt the color seep into me even before the rays began to warm the cold sands, and I remembered the strong brush strokes of his paintings. He made the oils work for him, transposing the inner visions of his mind to the canvas. His paintings were mirrors of his complexity, sometimes revealing in the bright and jarring colors the frustrations he would never speak out load. And when he found serenity in a day, he would move his easel to the porch and let that peace flow through his hand to the brush, and a soft and luminous scene would emerge to please him.

He was a believer in the old-fashioned virtues. Family, and respect due to elders, were not to be questioned. He had deep love for and confidence in his mother and a filial respect for the quiet and gentle man who was his father. He visited his parents often, measuring out the day's time so that he would have given to them and his own family the precious minutes that his crowded life permitted.

He loved beautiful things and could find beauty in the simplest of objects. His credo called for clean things, too, and even when the seat was out of whack in his car, the car itself was spotless. He had hurried to get it repaired after we returned from Philadelphia so that there could be no impairment in the otherwise well-kept old model he liked to have on hand along with a new car he enjoyed driving.

He liked to work, reveling in rising early and being on time and ready to earn his pay. He believed in giving a full day's measure to whatever the work and had risen in only two years to become foreman at the plant. He had been looking forward to the challenge of opening his own business and taking the chances a small businessman must take with a new start. He was ready to give notice at the plant, when the unexplained accident stopped all his dreams.

I remembered his dreams as I sat on the quiet beaches over those weeks. Remembered how he wanted to be able to give his wife and daughters the visible signs of success in this life. Remembered how he had dreamed about giving black people something to hang onto in the times we found ourselves. Remembered that he had never consciously hurt anyone with his dreams. Remembered how good a friend he had been.

It was impossible to look at the tangible evidence of the hours, weeks and years we had worked together with the fruit of that once dream of his. It was wrenching to put a hand on a clipping or touch a flag or try to speak to an audience. I tried it a couple of times and found that I expected him to be there to hold out the flag with me at the end of a presentation. He wasn't.

It was far easier to turn down invitations, to withdraw from the quest, than it was to hide my feelings of loss and bewilderment. Our speeches had always used plural pronouns --- we, our. How do you change that and say "I" when the dream was his to begin with? No, it was easy to pack it all away, the flag and everything associated with it, buried in boxes in my basement and forced into the far recesses of my mind. There was no way to deal with the overwhelming sense of futility and despair that shadowed every effort to continue to talk about the flag.

I made changes in my life, adjusting the pace and focus in painful increments day by day. I cut the grass so frequently and so exactly one would think a professional gardener had taken up residence with my family. Things that needed doing around the house got done quickly. I had time to look at my growing daughter and marvel at the seven year old that asked questions about the things she was learning in school. I'd stand in her bedroom door and watch her settle down to homework. She was a delight with a quick mind and a ready eye to see the world and to inquire about it.

I listened to my favorite records often, sitting in the recroom downstairs, just sitting and doing not much thinking.

I found that everyone in my personal life had changed while all my energies had been focused on the flag. They had grown, begun to find interests that absorbed them. My wife had developed a strong attachment to the women's lib movement and belonged to a group that met regularly to discuss the issues that were beginning to emerge. My parents had grown older, my father retired, still strong, but older and more fragile in some indefinable way. My mother was still the pillar of strength she had always been, but now she was no longer working, spending her time exclusively in the house and at the church. Only two years and everyone had charted a course that took us down separate paths.

I didn't look for things to occupy my time outside home. It was more quieting to just go to work everyday, come home to chores around the house, spend more time with the family and see my parents more frequently. Still, when a friend came by one evening and talked about a youth group he had started I was fascinated by the excited way he described the boys in the group and the things they were doing. Clyde was a rare one in the community. A newcomer to the area, he gave time to kids in ways that few seemed prepared to do.

The group he described was composed of boys between fifteen and seventeen, about twenty-five of them. They met twice a month, using a room in the YMCA in Elizabeth for their meetings and in those sessions they tried to discover ways to organize themselves to become more politically aware, more socially conscious of themselves and their environment, and to share their aspirations for the uncertain futures they faced at the end of the decade of the sixties.

The group had formed in one of those happenstance ways that sometimes occur. Clyde had been working out regularly in the gym at the Y and had developed friendships with a few of the boys who were there for sports activities. Casual conversation led to the decision to form a group with the focus imbedded in the name they chose, Youth Leadership Club. The group was not affiliated with any organization; it was just one of those circles that spring up from the fortuitous meetings of people with common interests.

Clyde described the activities the youth group and he had begun, the plans to bring in speakers, and the teen dances and cake sales and raffles the boys wanted to run to raise funds to pay for the calibre speakers they wanted. An adult board of directors had been formed. He asked whether I would be interested in working with him, helping make contact with potential speakers, supervising fund-raising activities, and sitting in on rap sessions that occupied much of the formal meetings. He didn't need to remind me of the environment from which the boys came. I knew it first hand. Most were being raised in one-parent households; the places they called home were the mean shelters of the black impoverished. Working with these boys sounded good. If Clyde could volunteer his time to a group of young black males who wanted to hone themselves in preparation for making a good life later, so could I.

I went to the first meeting and sat quietly while the personalities of the boys began to emerge. I could see the frustrations of being young, black, poor and oppressed in the faces of Gary, Smitty, Gil, Richie, Guy and the others whose names I soon learned as the twice-monthly meetings took place.

They were a diverse group with aspirations that, would take them into professional acting and photography and pro-sports in just a few years. But for now, they were searching for assistance in understanding self and society that for too many young black teens was never available. They needed to know that black men could achieve in some way, bring some distinction to themselves, earn a place in the world that would move them far from their neighborhoods.

They were ambitious, tugging at almost non-existent bootstraps, wanting to work, wanting to free themselves of the trap that the city enclosed them in, trying to understand where the chaos of the '60s would lead.

The opportunity to work with those boys was a curious detour in my life. I chose to work with them; yet, it was almost as though it was meant to be in some grand master plan. As they asked their questions about their existences, their lives, their neighborhoods, their relationships with the larger world, I was forced through introspection. I discovered the universality of experiences boys encounter as they grow up in the poorer parts of a sprawling urban community.

The boys in the Youth Leadership Club came from the midtown section of Elizabeth and hadn't lived in the Frog's Hollow of my childhood, that part of the city which nestled between two huge storage tanks of the Elizabethtown Gas Company down the south end of my street and the old red brick fortress-like buildings of the Singer Company at the other end. My childhood community lay almost at the river in the Elizabethport section of the city, detached from the major arteries, and valuable only for an underpaid work force for the city's industries.

My world was confined to the boundaries the school, our church and my father's workplace created for me. It was a largely Polish neighborhood of wood frame houses. Black families lived in fourteen or fifteen of the small, old, grey houses packed in close to each other. Four families used the single toilets in the hall on each floor outside the cold water flat that was home. Six or seven steps led up to the porch that wrapped around the front and right hand side of our house. A front door opened into the long hall that divided the two ground floor apartments and the stairway leading up to the small second floor apartment we lived in. The bannister on that stairway was worn and unpainted.

Our four-room apartment was close, tight quarters for the five of us --- my parents, my brother, sister and I. My parents had a bedroom, my brother and I shared the other, my sister slept in the living room on a fold-out couch. There was no central heating. The kerosene stove in the kitchen did double duty as cookstove and source of heat for the whole apartment. My brother and I took turns going to the basement where kerosene was stored, filling a jug and bringing it upstairs to be placed in a rack by the stove so we could be assured of constant heat in winter and for cooking. The kitchen was turned nightly into a bathroom after dinner and dishes were done. The galvanized tub would be pulled off the wall and filled with water heated on the stove. We took turns bathing and refilling the tub for the next one. My parents insisted on cleanliness. The curtains at the living room windows were pulled down regularly and washed and ironed meticulously, even during the winter. Mother couldn't tolerate dirt and it was always a struggle for me when my turn came to lug the tub upstairs to the attic so that she could hang the family wash on the line strung from the window out to the pole in the tiny backyard of the house.

The attic was an extension of the apartment. Old clothes and newspapers were stored there to wait for spring when my father loaded them into the car to take to the junkyard. My friends and I played hide and seek during the winter months in the dim light of the one bulb strung overhead or sometimes sat quietly with a checkerboard until late in the afternoon when I'd hear my mother calling up the steps to tell me to bring in the wash line.

The four rooms and the attic were my home, the place where the Georgia-born man who was a foundry worker and the domestic worker who was my mother, raised the three of us in a stern and loving way, insisting on music lessons on the piano in the living room, school lessons at the kitchen table, prompt and regular readiness for church on Sunday, and tolerating no defiance or disobedience through all the days of my childhood.

I never wanted to run away, from home like some of my friends talked about doing. They lived in the same kind of house, trotted down similar dark hallways to the toilet, slid bannisters the same way I did. But, they didn't seem to have the urge to rise above the environment, to fight it with determination and deep resolve.

When the Youth Leadership Club began to plan a fund raising effort for its 1970 Conference I was brought back full circle to the flag. Impressed by what they were planning, I decided to seek donations from friends. One person I approached was Dave Topf. He wanted to know about the club and what I was doing with the flag. Hearing that the club was trying to make things happen pleased him. He wasn't convinced when I told him I had put aside the idea of the flag when Gleason died.

I had met Dave Topf in tenth grade when I went looking for work. I asked him to let me work in his shop for a day so he could see what kind of worker I would be. He told me to come back the next day and he would give me a try. Early the next morning I was standing in front of the shop when Dave arrived. He kept me on the job until I finished high school.

Dave waited quietly as I gave slow answers to his questions about the flag. He finished off the cool drink he was having, leaned forward in his chair. "You're going to need some help when you get ready to give the flag another try. Give me a call when that time comes."

He had offered help. I was going to take it.

Chapter 7

The night was sultry and we had escaped to the basement recroom where it was cooler. After a few minutes my daughter decided to go upstairs to her favorite books and soon my wife followed her and I was left alone, sitting deep in my favorite chair, lights dimmed, music playing softly.

The conversation with Dave Topf had thrown me into a state of confusion that I had not shared with my family. I needed to just sit and let the music take over my consciousness for a while and then it might be easier to think through what we had talked about.

The records dropped one after another on the turntable, filling the basement with sounds that wiped away all thoughts of the world outside. The driving gospel bass line of Billy Taylor's "I wish I Knew How It Would Feel To Be Free" reached out and grabbed hold of me. The melody, hypnotic in its simplicity, lay on top of the bass and drums. Soon I was humming with the music, then singing it, then thinking about the words.

How does it feel to be free? How might it feel to be both black and free? How would it feel to be free of the need to see the flag recognized and accepted? How can I make the flag wave freely wherever black people are?

Dave had spoken so quietly tonight, so surely about what the flag meant to me. He knew that somehow it would not be left to lie, a fallow and forgotten thing that once was and was no more. And he was right. If the flag had meant something , anything, to me in the past then it was impossible to lay it aside and walk away from it. But, what could be done now?

How was it to happen again? How would it be different now that picking it up once more would depend solely on me?

My life was different, things had changed. My job, took me into New York City daily, leading me through the mazes of an entirely new and exciting challenge to create displays for a retail record company. Days were filled with traveling between the company's stores, setting up or dismantling displays, designing layouts for presentations when new recordings were to get heavy play, checking on the progress of the two assistants who worked under me. I had responsibility, authority, a sense of creative juices flowing freely in that world. My time was not constricted by a clock; I could linger in out-of-the-way display houses looking for some special unique props that would make my windows distinctive. The people who inhabited that world were different from anyone I had known before. They moved rapidly, spoke a clipped language that was peculiar to the trade, nuances clear to the record cutters, distributors, store managers, promoters. A work day was busy, full of movement and activity that kept me on a plane of challenging work that was interesting and exciting. No two days were alike, no two places were the same, and no man told another man's jokes --- at least, not on the same day.

The rhythm of everyday life settled into predictable patterns of work and evenings free to spend with my family.

And there was the youth group to look forward to, working through their expectations for the social changes that would give them the open door to fulfill their dreams. They talked, intensely, when a black Congressman on television commented on new legislation. The boys wanted to know whether the initiatives of blacks in Congress stood a chance, whether the words that poured out in interviews would make a dent in the attitudes of the American people, white Americans, and provide any greater hope for better lives for them.

We had met the night before to work on details for the Youth Leadership Conference they were sponsoring soon. They sat in a loose circle in the bare room in the YMCA that was the meeting place. The metal chairs hardly contained the large frames and gawky legs of the taller boys and they sat with hands folded over knees bent upward and out over feet that traveled so confidently over miles of basketball court that was home, playground and training field for some of them.

"Do the initiatives of black people stand a chance?" Their question had no easy answer. We were in a backwater of the civil rights movement; other events were beginning to overshadow the memories of the violence and turmoil of the '60s. Vietnam was no longer a distant war site; the issues it spawned were clogging the television screens. American sensitivities were still trying to recover from the laser beam attack of incivility unleashed at Kent State University only a few months before. Women were gathering themselves into a political force that generated steam from conversations over kitchen tables and cold coffee. They grappled with abortion, affirmative action, and the art of politics. Black people were off the streets and into the conference rooms were proposals for grant money were being written to support the programs that were thought necessary for someone, somewhere.

Whose initiatives did stand a chance? It seemed that just anybody's initiatives could find a willing ear. The Supreme Court stood ready to deal with practically any issue of social significance, taking to itself many of the everyday decisions that had been handled in local communities for hundreds of years. Changes in the social fabric were woven each day as Courts and Congress dispensed first social ideology and then the "title" money to support it.

Yet, things were not different. Black people were not making too many initiatives in their hometowns. A handful of black men sat in mayor's offices around the country trying to learn how to hold the reins of power on even that limited basis. Unemployment rates were high, as always, for blacks; our young men were dying in disproportionate numbers in Vietnam; our children were pawns, moving at the Court's will across the district lines of their neighborhood school. As desegregation replaced integration, yellow buses carrying black students passed yellow buses carrying white children to the schools in black neighborhoods. The cry for justice had resulted in meager signs of progress and more in displacement, dislocation and dysfunction. If things were better for black people, it was hard to find evidence in my hometown or in any black neighborhood where poverty and misery still characterized the way of life. People were wondering when peace and prosperity would appear while drugs destroyed dreams and bent minds into shapes beyond the ken of society. We seemed hell-bent to destroy ourselves on the battlefields of some alien land and to sap the potential millions of young people in the name of a inner space trip at home.

The boys in the group were not drug-users, yet, they were traumatized by the absence of a sense of personal worth in the times. They talked about their sense of manhood, the need to affirm the worth of their potential in ways that were productive and positive. Their questions were thoughtful, not rhetorical.

"Why does my blackness deny me a chance? Why does being black affect every little move I make? Why can't being black sometimes give me an edge in a good way? Why does it hinder me before I can even begin to live? Why women's liberation when I am not yet free? Why do I have to go and die in Vietnam? Why will I get no further than my parents got in life? Why?"

Their faces were earnest and troubled. They were looking to the adults in the room for answers. What do you say to young black men, teenagers who are thinking and striving but seeing already the futility of trying to better themselves? The world outside was complex, its events beyond easy answers to explain the origin or ultimate disposition of those events. There was no magic wand that would make the problems of being black disappear anymore than the conflict in Vietnam could become a big picnic for their older brothers who were already there.

I had already traveled the passage from child to man, asked my questions of others and gotten no answers and so, had to reach inside myself to know why I could continue to climb up and out of the seventh ring of Hell that was being black in America. For what it was worth, I had shared with them the only answers I knew.

"Why do you dwell on the impossibilities you think you face? Why don't you look inside yourselves to find the source of power that will turn things around for you. You have it; it is the gift of history that is part of your blackness, part of your heritage. It's been refined in the smelter's fire that has been our history. The strength you're seeking to break the chains is inside you. It is the same strength that made survival possible. It's knowing that you are a person of worth and taking pride in that fact. It's knowing that you can take responsibility for yourself and others and can meet the challenges that you will have to face. It's knowing who you are and not being afraid to share that sense of identity with others and finding a way to wear your blackness without fear or shame. It's discipline, inner discipline, that kneads your mind and muscles to prepare you to meet your challenges and gives you the surge of energy when it's needed, discipline that tells you to make no move without considering the aftermath of that move, discipline that makes you lay aside the lure of the easy way out and to try instead to make your mark on history in the bold strokes of an artist at life. It's making the effort to create a better world instead of moaning about how horrible life is.

"Children moan and cry out against the terrors of the night; adults turn on a light to chase away those terrors. You have to do the same thing. Find some way to lighten the load, the burden that black people have carried all the generations of our lives in this country. You have to do it if you would call yourselves men."

The boys sat very still as the words tumbled out of me, listening intently as the words that defined the black man for me were spoken again. Pride, responsibility, identity, discipline, effort. A black man was obligated to find some personal credo and to let it mark his every thought and action.

They listened closely, their faces showing their inner efforts to come to terms with the statement. The meeting ended soon after. They left the hall with hands thrust in pockets and heads hung in thought. Maybe it had been too tough to tell them that they would have to look within to find their answers. But that's the way it was.

That's how it had been for me. Wasn't I obligated to act on the word *effort*? Was it not necessary for me to lay aside the lure of a comfortable, predictable life that had its pleasures and rewards and pick up again the threads of the flag's fabric? Dave had been right. If there had been a reason for the flag in 1967, the same reasons still existed only three years later. The painful questions asked by the boys told me in the plainest of words that the needs of black people were still not met, that the shame of blackness overwhelmed the potential that it cloaked instead of giving that potential a burnish to make it stronger. Their questions and Dave's certainty that an effort would be made again drove me deeper into the night, sitting alone and feeling my way through what might happen next.

Whatever could happen with the flag would be vastly different from all that had gone before. Where once there had been two of us to unfurl a banner, there was now only one. If things were to happen they would have to come solely from my own initiative. And from non-existent resources, resources depleted except one -- an idea that sometime, somehow, black people could grasp the significance of a symbol that, in this nation of ethnics, would serve as a rallying point to illustrate their consensus of pride and purpose.

I was sure that consensus was there, buried under the burden of accumulated shame and self-pity that made us prey to the manipulation of others. It would emerge one day in a generation of black people who would stand up and be counted among those for whom life had purpose and meaning and for whom the worth of a man was measured not in the color of his skin but in the power of his mind and the soaring strength of his spirit. It would be measured in the accomplishments of a new generation of young black people who could ask questions to plumb the depths of self-knowledge and swim out of that compelling experience to find themselves purified through defined blackness and pride in self.

If the flag did nothing more than stir people to talk about blackness and its meaning, then it would prove its worth.

How was that to happen though? How were people to know of its existence? What had to be done?...and where?...and how?... and with what?

I stirred in my chair, realizing that it had been hours since that conversation with Dave and that I had nothing to go with, not the faintest idea of where to start again.

Chapter 8

D ave and I talked in the weeks after that conversation. He provided a sounding board for my frustration at the two years spent working with the flag. It was true that the basic premises of the flag were as valid now as they were in the beginning and that thousands of people were aware of it, but that was not enough. Without question, the flag had to be seen by masses of black people for its symbolism to acquire meaning and value.

"How do you reach millions of people?" I asked Dave, knowing that he had no easy answer for me.

He threw the question back, "How does anybody do it? How did the automobile get to be the consuming symbol of adulthood in this country? Somebody made a good product; it advertised itself, then somebody else got the bright idea of deliberately stimulating people to buy the thing. We've been hooked on cars ever since."

"But how do you get people hooked on a symbol that you can't ride or put on your back?"

"Mel, you will have to find that way. You can't sit still and expect to find a line of people at your door one day, queued and waiting for their issue of symbolism. You will have to find a way to grab attention, get some media exposure, find some sponsor to help you get that media attention. That's how you'll have to reach all the people you will want to reach."

How simple and easy that sounded. Somebody had suggested once that the best way to get to a whole lot of black people was to become a religious leader, built your own little sect, plant cells in every city, cells organized and mobilized around your credo, then you ordered them to unfurl the flag at every house and meeting hall. If you were persuasive enough as you massaged their religious needs, you could pull it off. Dave laughed at that and said he didn't think I'd make a good evangelist.

A reporter told me once that the flag could get all the television and newspaper time it could use if there were a threat to burn down a major city or a body was found somewhere with the flag draped around it. That would lead to all the media coverage in the world; flashbulbs would pop as you were hauled off to jail with the flag wrapped across your shoulders. That would be publicity you could treasure while you measured the days of your life in little scratch marks on a cell wall!

Those were useless thoughts. I was no evangelist, nor was I an arsonist or murderer. The flag had to be brought to public attention with dignity, grace, and unblemished record and history. It was time to think, to analyze, to plan for a means to make the dream of the flag become reality.

In our conversations it soon became evident that a major problem was that of financial resources to mount a public relations effort that would somehow reach out to the black population in positive and productive ways reflecting the seriousness and dignity that the flag represented. Dave agreed that a professional in public relations or advertising, might be the key that Gleason and I had not found and we made our way through the word-of-mouth campaign earlier.

Once our talk turned to my job and the kinds of people with whom I worked. Dave thought that perhaps someone might lead me to a reputable and effective public relations man. He would flip through his mental card file to see if a lead surfaced. That we agreed on the importance of securing a competent leg-man and that there might be possibilities within our acquaintances was stimulating and encouraging. How such a competent person would be paid was still a problem, but then, if the right person was not found, then money was no concern. That was the one thing that had been haunting me and causing me to hold back from making an outright commitment to resume work with the flag.

Dave remarked once that it would be necessary to give any renewed effort one-hundred percent of my time. I looked at him for a long moment. He said it calmly, almost casually. What havoc that would cause in my personal life, the disruption in the steady rhythm that had built up in the last year, a rhythm that gave me more time to spend with my wife and daughter and parents, to do more household tasks, to work in the community at a leisurely pace. Just how could I go full-time with the flag and still support my family? But, he was right. This was what haunted me --my need to give one hundred percent.

The question was hypothetical at that point though. Talk and more talk about what was needed had occupied all our conversations. There had been no commitment to do anything more than be alert to opportunity approaching the doorstep. No ad for a public relations man appeared in any newspaper. No organization was approached for endorsement. There had been nothing but talk. But talk was important. Through those conversations with Dave, possible courses of action were refined and a growing sense of readiness to try again was beginning to absorb me completely.

After that last talk with Dave I felt at peace with myself. I had no idea how a new beginning would manifest itself, but it was coming. What changes it would force on my life were imponderable, but meeting a challenge was the measure of my personal worth as a human being. From that day, every encounter in the day's work was marked by watchfulness, a keen edge to each conversation. That edge would cut a beginning point for another try to awaken the people to the flag's existence.

My work was filled with an assortment of interesting people, men who had far-reaching contacts in the business world. It seemed that everybody knew somebody. Who you knew could put you on the fast track. But nobody had had experience dealing with a concept as unique as the flag. In a year when radicalism of antiwar factions in the country sometimes came down to the simple question of whether to burn the American flag at a rally, the surge of feeling for the country's banner overshadowed discussions with people I met in the run of a day. When it was possible to avoid juxtaposing the American flag with this one, it was necessary to listen for nuances that indicated empathy for black people. It was impossible to look for someone in public relations whose attitudes indicated no concern for a black symbol of pride. For weeks no leads that promised a willing ear.

Early in September of 1970 a chance conversation propelled me to the opportunity I had been seeking. One record distributors' office was a frequent stop as the Broadway play *Purlie* was being given heavy promotion. I needed album jackets for a display and stopped by the major distributor to pick up a few. This particular distributor and I sometimes talked about events in the city. On this day there was a lull in his morning. Over the coffee he offered, we got to talking about *Purlie*. He said it was good theatre; I thought it presented a slice of black life that was important for people to see --good theatre, good music, tremendous acting, or whatever. Before long we were discussing the growing numbers of blacks attending theatre. *Purlie* was the personification of black audiences' wishes and dreams. He wanted to know, "What dreams?" and "What wishes?"

"For peace. Prosperity. A slice of the American pie. A sense of dignity and self-respect. That's some of what black people want."

"I know what you mean, Mel, but those are things everybody wants so what makes them special dreams to black people?"

"They're special because they are almost impossible to achieve. Black people have to dream everything in color because color overshadows everything. In the make-believe world of the theatre, black people don't get roles that aren't color-cast, and in the real world, everything is judged by the color of the skin. It's so bad that if there isn't a sense of individual self-worth to pull you through, the black man feels as though he doesn't even exist. That's why the play is so important to blacks. They win, for once, on the stage. That sense of self-worth and the need to make it plain for all to see is why I spent a lot of time trying to push an idea out to black people that I thought could give them a better sense of self."

"What idea?"

We were into an intense discussion about the flag. His interest was obvious and it felt good to have a listener really listening and seemingly understanding what the flag meant to me. He wanted to know what had happened recently, what efforts were being made. It took another few minutes to tell him how the effort to do something was hanging free, waiting for someone to help it move out to the public. He thought for a moment and then asked if I would bring in a flag, some of the news articles, and whatever else was on hand that dealt with the flag. He wanted to see it and would give some thought to helping me find that elusive public relations person.

A couple of days later I dropped by his office with a box of clippings, brochures, decals and a flag, and we spent more time talking about the concept. Finally he turned the flag over in his hand and said he didn't have a name for me, but he would keep on thinking and get back to me. I wondered whether a polite stone wall had just been thrown up, but as usual, any discussion of the flag was energizing so it didn't seem a total loss of time.

A few days later he called, excitement in his voice. "Mel, here I've been thinking about somebody who could help you and coming up short while all the time, there's a connection for you sitting in my front office."

"Who? Who is the connection?"

"My secretary. Her boyfriend is in public relations. He's a musician and art dealer and knows people--hundreds of people. He stays on the move, but if you call her, she'll make the contact for you. You can at least give it a try. His name is Sam."

It sounded good. It was a lead, at last.

The secretary got hold of her busy boyfriend and he called me. She shared with him what her boss had told her about the flag and Sam was interested in meeting to talk about it. We arranged lunch--about a month later when his schedule was free enough.

Sam was waiting at the restaurant that Tuesday in early October. I had expected him to look like some centerfold type straight out of *Esquire*. The secretary was good-looking and any choice of hers would just have to have that Madison Avenue look. Sam was unexpected, a slender, almost thin, beige-skinned young man with the hint of an accent I couldn't place. Gradually, as we talked, the accent fell into a corner of my memory from Navy days. Sam was Somalian. The rhythm of his words was reminiscent of the East African coast.

Sam was as fast a talker as he was a mover and shaker in his world. From a loft on lower Madison Avenue, he distributed art reproductions to dealers. His phone jumped off the hook with calls from musicians wanting him for a gig, from his contacts in publishing, the theatre, and friends in the academic world. Sam seemed to know everyone and was difficult to pin down for any length of time. He thrived on not being in one place long, so it was amazing that he sat still to listen to a description of the flag and plea for assistance in finding a public relations man. We talked at length. We had a common understanding of the flag's merits. But Sam was never in one spot long enough to be any help to me.

It was a surprise then, one night when I returned home from a Youth Leadership Council meeting, that my wife told me he had called to say he was interested in the flag and wanted to help.

She was ambivalent after the call from Sam. The flag had been put to rest, she thought. My time would be spent at home, she thought. Her fears, well-hidden through the time Gleason and I had worked on the flag, surfaced that night. Fears that people would say I was crazy to pursue this thing, that the shunning she had seen begin in the early years would continue, intensify, erupt in some wild and dangerous moment that might end my life.

"People are afraid to get involved with you, with the flag. You're stirring up waves you can't calm down, Mel. Can't you see that you're asking for trouble?"

"What kind of trouble? What can happen?"

"You can wind up dead!"

So what! A black man is dead anyway if he doesn't find something to live for, something to give him hope for a better future, something to call his own in a world where nothing comes easily to anyone and least of all to those who are dispossessed at birth just because of color or race.

We talked for hours, she describing all the things I knew to be true. We were young, beginning to get a comfortable life together. We could live out our lives without fear, without dreading to come into the driveway where someone might be lurking in the bushes to beat you up. We could do this if I would let the flag stay packed away.

It was hard to cut through her talk, to try to convince her that it was not enough to have designed the flag, that until there was some measure of acceptance the design meant nothing, and that fears for personal safety were not enough to offset the need to pursue the ideal again. I could do little to dissipate her apprehensions. There was little to justify her fears, it seemed to me. Open threats had never been made against me. Friends who felt some disquietude at being associated publicly with me or the flag had snubbed us, but that was about all that might be construed as threats. Somehow she was certain of physical harm if I resumed, and her fears were real to her. The flag was more important to me.

The conversation ended, neither of us pleased with the outcome. My determination to plunge into another try was firmly in place. I knew it was driving a wedge between us. Each of us hoped that the other would understand and become supportive. She was gracious in the end, hoping that if the effort had to be, some good people would give me assistance.

When she went upstairs, I turned to think about what could happen if Sam found solid help for me. Going full-time with this would become reality. In that case, how would my family be supported? My brother, Bernard, might hire me for work in his custom cleaning service doing offices at night. I could work with the flag during the day and join one of his work crews at night and still be the family provider, but who wants to work for his brother? If nothing else came along, that would have to be it and my pride would just have to go in my back pocket along with a paycheck.

More compelling than worries about earning a living was figuring out what Sam could do to get the flag moving. So much time had gone into developing the hypothesis that all the flag needed was a good PR man. Now that one was on the horizon, what would he do? How could he grab the kind of thoughtful attention that was required from a lot of people? And, where would the resources come from to support the whole effort?

It was almost impossible to deal with imponderables when you have been alternating between exhilaration of doing what you really want to do and the despairing reality of demands on time, money, and personal relationships that would follow.

Days later, Sam gave me an outright, powerful jolt. *He* would work as PR man for the flag!

He shot that down just as quickly as he spoke the words, "Hey Mel, I'm always on the go. I may pull out one day, any day. When things are moving someplace I gotta go where they are. That's me, my man."

He was matter-of-fact. He was fascinated by the flag but hooked on his own life style. It wasn't exactly take it or leave it, but it came so close that it was unnerving. Sam recognized the emotion he saw in my face and he came back with an appeasing declaration that made me feel much better. If the day came that he knew he would leave to check out other pastures, he would be sure to connect me with someone else so things would not bottom out.

I believed him. Sam was honest and straight-forward and that made it easy to deal with him.

We met frequently for several weeks, reviewing great detail the first round with the flag. He wanted to know everything, the contents of unsolicited mail, what had happened at the conferences, churches, meetings, interviews that made up the first attempt at promoting the flag. He soaked it up for future reference, asked question after question.

Sometimes we scheduled meetings and he didn't show. A couple of days later he would call and say he'd been out of town on a deal, and then he'd launch into a continuation of the last conversation we had had.

One day close to Christmas, Sam dropped the word. He was shipping out of the city. As he promised at the outset, he was going to give me a connection. The man was financial advisor, smooth, smart, well-versed in his art, and ready to meet with me. His name was Lee Winkler and Sam would arrange for us to meet at Winkler's office before the week was out.

As he described Lee Winkler and his contacts, my excitement grew. Not only was Sam keeping his promise to deliver a new connection, but it sounded like a real winner. We hung up on Sam's word that he would call with a specific meeting time, that he would have filled in Winkler even more than he'd already done, and that things were moving for me.

"1971 is going to be a good year for you and the flag, Mel, sure as my name is Sam!"

That kind of certainty felt good. The feeling lingered right through the holidays while Sam disappeared on one of his gigs and gave me no sure date for the meeting with Winkler.

Right after New Year's Day, Sam called. The appointment was set. "Wednesday, 10 o'clock, Mel. See you there."

Chapter 9

Winkler's office was on Fifth Avenue, midtown and elegant. The double Gothic doors, the fashion-plate receptionist, the French provincial chair and the crystal ashtray, signaled high-powered people accomplishing with ease and certainty. Waiting for Sam, I looked at the mirrored walls, plants with shining leaves, the gold and red color scheme, and thanked the gods of fortune for a promising beginning.

Sam had not arrived when the receptionist told me in a low, clear, professional voice to go into Mr. Winkler's office. My attache case seemed suddenly very light as I wondered whether there was enough of anything in it to interest him. Winkler had to be used to dealing with moneyed people and this was the errand of a man begging for help.

A tall, broad-shouldered man with grey-black hair, dressed quietly fashionable, rose to greet me from behind a French Provincial desk. His hand, ringed in gold and diamonds, was extended as the smooth voice welcomed and invited me to sit, get comfortable, and tell him about the flag.

His confidence wrapped him like the sheen on the table I used to spread out the paraphernalia of the flag. I felt his attention directed totally to the thing. He was direct. It was important to find out how I had come to know Sam. While answering, a corner of my mind nudged me to ask how he knew Sam. The circle of acquaintances was business-originated. Winkler was immersed in the theatre world. Sam had favorably impressed many people.

We talked for about twenty minutes. Whether at his office, on the phone, or out for an occasional drink at the end of the day, each new encounter with Winkler was brief and to the point.

He put us on a first-name basis in that meeting after delving into the history of the flag and determining that I was sincere and honest about what had brought me to him. Later, it became clear that his confidence came from his ability to cut through to the core of the business and the person presenting it. If either were shaky, Lee had no time to give.

Sam breezed in as we neared the end. He and Lee greeted each other warmly and sat down to hear me wind up the flag's history. Lee sat a moment looking at the flag. Finally he thanked me for coming and reiterated his understanding of my plea for assistance. He made no outright offer of assistance, but I felt he was comfortable with what he had heard.

Sam and I left together. He took off into the morning crowd without word of Lee's reaction to my presentation. Sam called later that evening. "Lee likes you. He wants to see what he can do to help." Hearing those words was pure relief. Maybe something was going to happen after all. I wanted to know what Lee was going to do to help.

Sam's response indicated that Lee himself would let me know by arranging another meeting. If Lee's usual pattern was at work, there would be something of interest waiting for me.

A week later, Lee called to set a time for the meeting. I let Sam know, and he promised to be there. He wasn't. In fact, Sam dropped off the scene totally, just as he had said. There was never any further word from him.

Lee and I met at his office. He came directly to the point. He had thought about the nature of the flag and decided that it required the know-how of those who manufactured advertising specialties. The essential move was to get the flag into products that were inexpensive, easy to acquire, and appealing to all age groups. He would talk with manufacturers in the city--people who made flags, t-shirts, campaign-type buttons--to find someone who could see the financial benefit of holding an exclusive contract to produce the items. He asked again about the patent rights, to assure the patent had devolved to me exclusively. Once again, I told him that was the case, that my lawyer confirmed that when the records of the defunct GleaMel Enterprises were examined. Lee proposed drawing up a contract giving exclusive production and manufacturing rights for perhaps a year to the "right" businessman that he would find. He made it clear that while finding that "right" person would be his move, my task was to convince the businessman of the project's validity and of my own sincerity. If product and person passed the critical inspection, the right people would take the project and it just might fly.

That meeting was powerful. The world of financial advisory unfolded before me. Lee had listened to a concept, explored it for intrinsic worth, then examined it for financial worth. Once locked in, he decided which contact button to push to produce the desired results. He decided that mass exposure of the flag in a variety of forms was the answer. "Produce the item, then promote it."

Lee promised to get back to me as soon as he found a manufacturer sensitive to the project and willing to get involved in the social and the production end. In the meantime it was important for me to plan a presentation that would grab and hold attention.

January ended without my hearing from him. The winter was cold, roads snowy, and in the long drives from home to my job, I had lots of time to think about what needed to be said once Lee turned up the right people. It never crossed my mind that he might fail in that search. His aura of confidence denied the possibility of failure.

Many mornings while driving in to work, I thought of the experiences Gleason and I had had, the people we met, the places we visited, the rejections when we were denied that home-town unfurling of the flag, the elation when Newark had shown it had guts. The faces of black people who wanted a cut when we had only a concept to offer, the woman who summed up the game-playing that passed for black politics in Boston, the delegates to the conferences who had spoken favorably about the flag, and the leaders who had denied the opportunity for group affirmation of its worth with me every day for weeks.

Should I tell a white businessman of the denials I had received from your own people? Would it profit him to know that friends avoided being seen publicly in my company? Did he even need to know that the flag was the symbolic affirmation of self-worth that my parents had drummed into me from birth, or that I felt I was making the contribution NAACP leaders and Urban League directors talked about on Sunday afternoons at church so long ago?

Or did he need to know that the flag was unwilling black immigrants, dispossessed, dispersed from a homeland, deprived of every link to a heritage worth honoring, stripped of knowing who they are?

It seemed best to focus on pride in self and race despite all. That ought to make him see the meaning of the flag. And, if it were necessary to sell myself as well, the focus would have to be on the truth --- that it was impossible to march alone, the resources were exhausted. I needed help to raise the flag higher on the rigid pole of black consciousness.

Whoever he was, wherever Lee was going to find him, he would have to understand what the flag meant to me and why I came with it in my hands to him. If that didn't do it, nothing could be said or done that would ever make things happen.

Lee called in early February. He had found someone after spending weeks talking with manufacturers who turned thumbs down on the project on a purely racial basis. Lee corrected himself and said "racist" basis. They hadn't wanted to learn anything about the flag or its history once it was identified as black in origin and for a black audience. Any money made from producing items was not sufficient inducement. But, Joe Zavlik was interested in listening, at least. A meeting was set for the next week at Lee's office.

Not long after my arrival, Zavlik strolled into the anteroom, unhurried, smiling, moving his compact frame around with assurance. His eyes were friendly, sparkling, and set me at ease almost at once.

This meeting was longer than any since the second effort started. Joe's unhurried attitude was deliberate; he gave himself plenty of time to decide whether to get involved. He sat quietly through the presentation that had shaped itself during the drives to and from work. He asked only a few questions, probing the early days of the flag particularly and the reasons for my resumption of the effort. He appreciated my flat statement that being a novice at marketing was my biggest stumbling block. His acceptance of that led me to believe that he saw some possibilities in the project.

We talked license, patent, contract parameters. For a while he sat back with the black portfolio holding news articles, letters, and pictures. He took his time reading each letter, each article. As he read, I thought about the portfolio he was holding, the same one that Gleason had given me several years before. It was quiet in the room as Joe read and I remembered again Gleason's words, "This is history, brother." It was! If there were ever to be more, the binder chronicled the early history and would serve as the starting point for the rest of the story.

When Joe finished reading, he put the portfolio on the coffee table and took up the flag that lay there. He examined it a few moments then rose, ending the session.

"I'll give you a call in a couple of days. How do I contact you?"

"You can call Lee. He'll reach me."

Joe left smiling, walking slowly to the door. He turned again to say, "You'll hear from me in a couple of days."

As the door closed, Lee told me to sit down again; we needed to talk some more. He was right: I needed to talk about the meeting. I wanted to know from him how it had gone and what were Joe's chances.

Lee was positive, upbeat. Zavlik was the right person. He had widespread connections with manufacturers and Lee was sure the presentation had interested him.

"You're going to hear from Joe. When he calls it will be to say that he is interested. You can trust him to get you moving on course and he will be fair in whatever contractual arrangements you will have to work out."

It sounded too good to be true. I wanted to give a shout and then realized that the elegant office would not ever have heard the kind of whoop I would have given. I just reached over to shake Lee's hand, "Thanks. We'll see what happens."

Lee couldn't possibly have known how much self-control it took to get those words out so quietly and calmly. The world was suddenly very bright. I had a feeling that this meeting with Joe Zavlik was turning point in the search for the right path.

A call came from Lee. It had been a busy week for me at work, preparing displays for the February holidays, setting up designs for Spring promotions. Keeping busy gave me little time to wonder when Joe would respond and even less to weighing what would follow from his call. A call came from Lee. His certainty that Joe was interested was enough to float me through work with an invigorated attitude.

Lee opened the conversation lightly. "Christmas has come again, Mel. Joe is interested and wants to work with you. Call him at his office, make your appointment and go on down there to hear what he has to say."

"Thanks, Lee. That's the best news of my life. Where's the office?"

"33rd street, across from Macy's, in the arcade."

"Ok, I got it."

"Well, my boy, lots of luck. "Lee was off the phone just that quickly. He wasted no words as he opened a door to the most exciting and demanding time of my life.

The call to Joe yielded an appointment for the next day. Joe manufactured novelties, advertising specialties made to order for hundreds of buyers. His office was a cornucopia of balloons, samples of emblems and t-shirts strung up on every inch of wall space, shelves bulging with boxes and stacks of embroidered flowers, animals, miniatures of every conceivable object that human beings would want sewn onto their clothing. The place was colorful, vibrant, crowded, alive. It was worth riding the shaky elevator up three stories to enter.

Joe greeted me at the door to his inner office after I had walked through the anteroom brimming with the products of his company. He offered coffee, a seat, and a stimulating half hour centered on developing a written agreement for us to work together. He didn't take many words to say he liked the idea of the flag, wanted to produce promotional items related to it, was opening his door for me to discuss it in detail with him, and that he would do all he could to make something good happen for me and for the flag.

His honesty and openness were reassuring and appealing. With someone else it may have been easy for me to wait for a hidden shoe to drop, for some agenda with all kinds of tricky items on it, but in the months that we would work together, Joe never dealt in chicanery or ulterior motives. He was a genuinely honest man and luck was with me. My response to him was as sincere as my gut feeling was strong. I thanked him for his interest and told him that it made me feel very good that he had chosen to work with me and the flag.

My need for a public relations man was the first thought put on the table. Joe thought we should take our time getting things organized on the manufacturing end, making sure that designs were properly developed for the several items we discussed. Once these were in place, we could set about securing whatever other assistance was needed. He felt that he could map out a strategy to promote the flag at that point.

He radiated confidence as he spoke so it seemed appropriate to hedge on the request for a public relations man and to put my eagerness on being overanxious to get everything done at once. He understood my sense of urgency and appreciated my reminder that I had been working with this idea for what seemed forever.

"Nothing is going to happen overnight, Mel. It taken careful planning and even more careful execution of those plans. Why don't you relax a little and just work with me while we go through all the details we have to get in place!"

He sounded like Dave Topf. Details! All right maybe it was better to ride at his pace. I needed him; he didn't have to get involved with me or the flag. This placid, pleasant man was successful in his business and he must know what he was doing.

We agreed that contacts with me would be through Lee's office and that we would continue legal arrangements within a few days.

Those arrangements took a little longer than expected. Once we met to have a drink after work. It was in that setting that he gave me insight into the widespread nonacceptance given to the flag by formal black organizations. He talked about merchandising, advertising, promotion and preparation when a new item headed for the mass market. As he described what went into developing a concept and its package in his business. I understood how essential it was to have a sense of timing and the ability to judge the right approach. It was late in the game to these basics, but it was good. At least it explained why the flag had not received the support and acceptance it should have gotten from organized groups. The idea had not been marketed in the right way. We had not operated on any principle of merchandising; rather, we had used only our sense of its meaning and value as its selling point.

As the days passed, Joe, my lawyer and I set up the contract to give him license to produce decals and emblems for a period of six months, with first refusal on renewal of the contract. Patent rights belonged exclusively to me and that there were no claimants to it. We drew up the contract and arranged for final review by all parties.

A few days before the scheduled signing of the contract. I called Gleason's widow, Miriam, and asked if I might stop by to see her for a few minutes. It was important to me that she knew I was beginning again with the flag and that she be given the opportunity to participate in it if she wished.

Our conversation was warm and cordial. We talked about her children and how much they had grown and reminisced about friends we shared. Finally, I told her that things were looking favorable for a second try with the flag and that if she wanted to be involved this time, her support and assistance and active participation would be welcome. She was gracious, as always, declining to take an active role. Her children were the focal point of her life and though she wished me well, she had no time to give to the flag.

Miriam knew well the energy and resources that had been expended earlier and sensed that this would require even more. It was not difficult to understand her reticence when April bounced into the room, needing Miriam's attention to some concern of hers. As they put their heads together, I thought of how much the child resembled Gleason and wished that he were there to see her growing so beautifully.

Miriam didn't know about my pilgrimage to his grave on Christmas morning, my first visit since his burial. The day was overcast, grey and cold. I left home very early, hoping to find a florist open so I could buy a grave cover. At the last shop, I peered into the window and knew there was no hope of buying a wreath, but out on the sidewalk in front of the shop was a stack of them, green leaves shining, red ribbons festooning the branches. I looked up and down the street; there was absolutely no one anywhere. I took a wreath, hoping there were no eyes to witness this theft. To make it right I'd have to come back later and pay for it, but for now this wreath was going to the cemetery with me.

There were a few people in the graveyard making their private pilgrimages. Miriam had planted a spreading evergreen near the stone and the grave was easy to locate. I placed the wreath on the stone and laid a small flag within its center. Then, believing that Gleason could hear me, I said, "Going to try one more time. This is something we wanted to do and I still believe in it. This is going to be my best shot at it. Rest easy, Pal."

As April and Miriam finished their discussion, my reverie ended. It was time for me to leave. Miriam walked with me to the door where she wished me luck. She asked again my understanding that she had to concentrate all her energies on the two children. I did understand and knew that this conversation with Miriam would close the past history of the flag. From here on out, there would be a new chapter, a fresh start with all the potential that emerging contacts in the world of business seemed to be offering.

Chapter 10

Joe Zavlik was central to all that followed in the next few months. Soon after we settled on the general terms of a contract he announced that he had friends who might be interested in producing other items that would help advertise the flag. He had a lawyer friend and a close associate who, he thought, would be a valuable part of a formal group to gain national attention. The lawyer, Vic Cozzi, was necessary to give in-house direction to decisions that would have to be made. The associate, Ted Shaw, was creative, analytical, quiet, constantly assessing product and market for the best match in advertising specialties. Ted and Vic could bring their special skills as well as provide capital. Ted's value would become even more evident as he created a network of several manufacturers who were to produce a wide variety of specialty items.

Joe set up a meeting with the two men for early March, acceding to my request that the session take place at Lee's office. That luxurious office seemed to vibrate with positive interaction and it was the preferred gathering place for me.

Both Joe and Lee indicated once again that a selling job on my part was required to get these men interested. Joe had talked with them in advance but, even so, my integrity and sense of purpose were on the line as openers for involving anyone in the project. As it turned out Lee was also on the line. Any time someone new entered the project, the entire past history of the flag had to be reviewed and everyone was subject to everyone else's scrutiny.

The meeting went well. Joe, Lee, Ted Shaw and Vic Cozzi talked about the project, the possibilities, the contractual arrangements, and ended with the usual "You'll hear from me soon." After Shaw and Cozzi left, Joe paced the room for a while. He was sure that the men were interested and would become actively involved, but there would be a waiting period. He thought that when these men decided to work with us we'd be able to move on getting a public relations man. If we timed it so that manufacturing of the products coincided with the development of a plan, we'd get to the successful marketing that was the end result we each were seeking.

He recognized that the flag would not move to the market without a thorough promotion campaign. We needed someone to steer that process. His thinking paralleled my own, and it was reassuring to hear him say this emphatically. I wanted to know where we could find someone to take on the charge of creating such a campaign. At that point Joe didn't know anyone who had the interest and the skills.

He was reassuring as he said again, "There's someone out there and I'll find him. Whoever it is has to be right for the work. We can't afford to make any mistakes in getting a campaign togethe,r and if we have to go slow until we find that man, that's what we'll do."

Lee chimed in, asking me to be patient and let things happen in the good time they were meant to occur.

Sometimes it is difficult to be patient. Staying in motion with the flag had dominated all of my earlier work. Coasting was in direct opposition to the style that had characterized the '67 - '69 period. Still, that very style might have been self-defeating. Cautious, careful planning and deliberate, calculated moves were necessary to success. The message seemed clearer and clearer. What worked earlier had met only limited success. If this effort were to be more effective, some of the methods of the past had to be discarded and new and different action plans had to be substituted.

In the meantime, the bottom dropped out of a huge chunk of my private life. I was fired from my job, though the company put it in more delicate terms. They said they were reorganizing.

March 1971 was tough! My family's reaction was pure shock. On the weekend after the lay-off notice, I decided to ask my brother to let me work for him. If Bernie agreed, I would work night for him and have days to pursue the project.

It's tough to ask an older brother to hire you. Almost any man would rather starve than ask for that kind of assistance. Starving was not my idea of fun though, so I asked and he agreed to try me. He would need to see how productively I could work with one of his cleaning crews before there would be real hiring. If I were late, inefficient or appeared to take advantage of being the boss' brother there would be grounds for dismissal at any time. If my work was satisfactory in every regard he would keep me on the payroll. Days became a blur of racing into New York for meetings with Joe and Lee, afternoons of cat-naps, early evenings of free-lancing. The office-cleaning assignment would last well into the early morning hours. A drive back home, a couple of hours of sleep and it would start all over again. I used to complete whatever display jobs came my way and to keep household chores below the panic line. Ted and Vic finally decided that they wanted in on the project. Ted and Vic, with Joe, organized themselves under the name Black American Associates, Ltd. (BLAM).

That contract gave them a six months exclusive license to use the flag design in the manufacture and sale of advertising specialties --- emblems, t-shirts, tie clasps, lapel pins --- for starters. The contract required the payment of royalties to me for the use of the license and gave them the right to sub-contract production of other specialties to any other manufacturer of their choice. Final approval of the use of the design on any item by anyone was reserved to me. A final clause gave BLAM the right to first refusal on a renewal of the contract at the end of the first six months.

It was definite forward movement for the flag, this contract, and that was an important step to me.

Just as things seemed to be falling into place, a shoe hit the floor with a crash. Lee was moving to California where a major portion of his clientele was concentrated.

That was devastating to me. Lee has been a source of support, a bulwark to lean against, a well-spring of information and guidance. He had become a mentor without charging a dime for his services. We had reached an understanding that if and when the project could be considered a success, he would receive a percentage of whatever income derived from the license and rights to the flag. He could have charged me by the hour. He never presented a bill to me.

He left New York with the assurance that he could be reached at his new office whenever needed. He urged me to maintain contact and let me know that when business brought him back to the City, he would be available to assist wherever and however he could.

On the evening that Lee left town I missed my first night of work for my brother. It was not a time to hustle a vacuum in some office in a skyscraper. I needed to consider the impact of Lee's physical separation from discussions and meetings and how the void created might be filled by my own efforts to communicate with Black American Associates.

Before all this was sorted out, my wife joined me at the kitchen table. We settled into another of the increasingly frequent discussions about time and energy being poured into the flag again.

This time she was direct in dealing with the issue of an ideal usurping so much time and attention. She said all the things we both knew to be true: Joy was growing and needed my active parenting, there were bills to be paid, friends were setting a pace in the community that was leaving us farther and farther behind, there was the lack of discernible progress in the pursuit of the ideal that needed an investment of time and energy that could go for a hundred years without yielding anything of substance -- neither recognition of the flag nor a sense of accomplishment for me.

I watched her as she talked, feeling the intensity of her thoughts as her words filtered through her near-tears. Everything she said was true, yet I wanted her to let me have that precious time and space to pursue this thing that was so important to me. I asked her to give me time, give me until the end of the year, let me have 1971 at least to prove that there could be growth, a flowering of the idea, a chance for recognition and acceptance of the flag.

She looked at me for a long time before she sighed a reluctant, "All right. The end of the year." She rose without any other words. I wondered how much more I could ask of her before this would all fall apart. Sleep was not easy that night.

The next night, back on the job, one of the men asked how one could be lucky enough to get the night off. We laughed about that, both knowing the ice was very thin under me where my brother was concerned. I told Ronnie about the need to take a breather to catch up on some things related to the flag. He wanted to know, "What flag?" And, we flew through the work that night with me doing most of the talking. Finally he said, "I think you feel about that flag the way I feel about playing my saxophone. If my music is going to be recognized, I'm going to have to keep working at it until somebody hears me play and wants more and more.

His enthusiasm, youthful and high-spirited, was good to see. He believed in himself and his music, believed in the picture in his head of a best-seller album with the name Ronnie Laws spread across the cover, believed that his dreams would become a reality and he would hear his music being played everywhere. We felt as strongly about our separate pursuits as it is possible for two men to feel and each of us understood what the other meant when he talked about his dreams. If he could know that he would succeed in a world where musicians stood on corners to be heard, then I could keep plugging away at my own dream. Thousands of musicians played the sax well, but there was only one flag. If he could beat the odds and make it, so could this flag!

Lee's move to California came in the spring of 1971 and he took the gathering steam. Joe, his associates, and I came to terms and began planning for production of several promotional items. We met frequently. In every instance, when a design was proposed, they honored the contract, deferring to me the final decision. Our sessions were usually brisk, short encounters arranged well in advance. Progress was being made, yet the meetings lacked forcefulness. We were focusing all attention on production considerations --- machinery, fabric, paper, packaging. No time was spent on the best means to reach the public.

Seeing the designs begin to stack up made me feel like I had on the day when I discovered the shelves of small Iraqi rugs in the ship's store. Nobody wanted to buy them. The same thing was beginning here; we were about to load up with something without first having stimulated the public's demand for it.

Joe's early musing on a public relations man was heard only rarely as he and the others focused more and more on production. I had counted on a public relations man. Joe, who was caught up in producing showed little inclination to take on the more important task of finding that expert. It fell to me, then, to bring up the issue again and again, to press the point that we had to stimulate demand, we needed a campaign to focus public attention on the flag.

The group acknowledged each time that here was a need, but the time was "not yet right." The sun was shining on the production of things, but we were making no hay in gathering attention.

This both pleased and distressed me. Some of this must have become apparent to Vic most particularly. Late in August, he and I talked about our general progress. That gave me an opening. I pressed him to explore his contacts, see who was available to help publicity. He must have asked around almost as soon as that little talk ended because it was only hours before he called to say he had a friend who might be able to work on the public relations end of the project. The friend was Jake Lamarr, head of construction division for one of the Rockefeller operations. Lamarr had an office on Avenue of the Americas and Vic arranged a time to discuss the flag. The meeting led to unexpected contact with the civil rights movement in the person of one of the more prominent of its leaders.

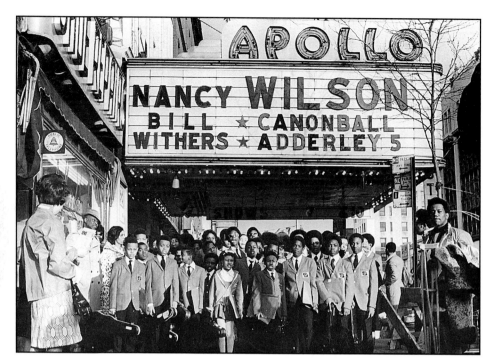

Ozanam Strings in front of the Apollo Theatre-N.Y.C.

Percy Sutton former Borough President of Manhattan displays the flag before the Ozanam Strings at City Hall in New York City.

Newark Raises First Negro Flag

3-11-68

LINDEN — The designers of a proposed flag for Black Americans have won their first victory in a campaign for national recognition of the banner.

The City of Newark hoisted the flag in front of City Hall in observance of Crispus Attucks Day. The Negro-American flag on a separate stanchion to the left of the American flag.

Melvin Charles of 1122 E. Henry St. and Gleason T. Jackson, 1517 Bower St., the designers, also are partners in a firm that would manufacture the flag.

They are seeking official recognition of the flag from Linden City Council, but have not received it so far.

Gleason and Jackson say they have received an estimated 2,000 letters from all parts of the country, as well as from Negro servicemen in Vietnam, as the result of news stories about the flag.

They claim the communications, almost without exception, express support of the idea of a flag to promote within black Americans a "unity of nationality and pride of history and tradition."

The designers emphasize that the flag is not intended to foster separatism. "We need the pride of a flag for our commemorative holidays," said Charles.

The holidays mentioned by Charles are in commemoration of the Emancipation Proclamation, Booker T. Washington, Medger Evers, Malcolm X, Crispus Attucks, the late President John F. Kennedy and the anniversary of the first slave to arrive in America.

Charles and Jackson contend that acceptance and recognition of the flag could help calm racial unrest by promoting pride in Negroes. People who riot and loot lack pride, they believe.

First newspaper article on the flag. (3-11-68)

One of ten original flags being presented to Dr. Nathan Wright at St. Augustine Church in Elizabeth, New Jersey. (From left to right) Melvin Charles, Dr. Nathan Wright, Gleason T. Jackson, Bob Blair.

Cannonball Adderley is presented with a Black American Heritage Flag at the Apollo Theatre by members of the Ozanam Strings.

Ambassador David Wilson of Liberia being presented with the Black American Heritage Flag from students touring the United Nations building in New York City.

Designer Melvin Charles tells the Springfield Mass. crowd about the history of the Black American Heritage Flag.

Melvin Charles unfurls the Black American Heritage Flag outside of East Orange City Hall in New Jersey.

Chapter 11

Jake Lamarr was in total command of his impressive office. The place had a fantastic view of the Manhattan skyline and narrow slice of the Hudson River. His office was at the end of a long corridor of offices, each a scene of bustling activity as secretaries moved in and out of conferences with the men who managed the construction of prefabricated houses that was the mainstay of the business. This was the scene of some high-powered activity in both labor and construction. Jake, broad-shouldered, brown-skinned, was the pipe-smoking boss.

It was a pleasure to meet Jake Lamarr. Vic introduced Joe, Ted and the project to him. The presentation flowed by now as easily as taking a breath of air.

Lamarr seemed to enjoy the history of the flag. He puffed on his pipe slowly as he asked what I thought he could do to help.

"The project needs someone of national stature to help focus attention on the flag, somebody who has access to the machinery that moves ideas out to the public. It needs somebody who can move the idea faster than I've been able to do on my own."

"What do you want me to do specifically?"

"Help us find someone, if not a civil rights person, then a damn good public relations man who will pick it up and run as far and as fast as he can." Holding his pipe, Jake leaned back in his seat. He threw out the name of Charles Evers, Medgar Evers' brother. Evers was in New York frequently and might be interested. Without pausing after the mention of Evers, he suggested Jackie Robinson, then Floyd McKissick. These men he knew and could contact easily.

Vic seized the moment and invited him to join BLAM. Jake smiled and said he was interested in doing whatever he could. He would work with us! Jake Lamarr was going to be a distinct asset!

We felt that this was the most productive meeting in a long time. We were on the road to filling a major gap that had existed in everything that had preceded that day. The feeling deepened when Jake promised to make contact with Evers and Jackie Robinson.

Two weeks later, we convened again at his office, impatient to hear what had transpired in the interim. Jake came to the point immediately. He had talked with Evers, shown him a flag, news articles and other regalia. Evers was definitely interested and willing to work with us. Jackie Robinson was in failing health and there was no energy to give to the project.

Jake couldn't have known how disappointed I was to hear that. Somewhere in the back of my head had been the hope that the old boyhood hero would materialize in the room and give the flag his endorsement and active support. Just the mention of his name had made me smile, taking me back to the long-ago days in Frog's Hollow when we played stickball and baseball in the field and pretended that we were Jackie, Campanella, and Newcombe. Heroes were few and far between for little black boys in my growing up days. Jackie Robinson had provided that image of guts and success, patience and pursuit of a goal that inspired and challenged. Jackie Robinson was more than a ball player to me. He was a hero in the classic sense of the word, slaying dragons, conquering mountains, winning laurels, and typifying everything a black man could be and do.

That Robinson was too ill to participate in the project was a disappointment. Had he been physically able he would have given his support to a concept that spoke of pride, effort, discipline, identity and responsibility. Jackie would have understood each word, known that the flag was a symbol of the achievements he had made as well as the aspirations and hopes that had been vested in it from the moment of its conception.

It was encouraging when Jake went on to describe Charles Evers' interest and the expected positive response from Floyd McKissick. When McKissick's name was mentioned this time , I told the group that he already knew about the flag, that we had met at a civil rights rally. Jake was interested in hearing about that meeting and my retelling of it took us off track for a while but he wanted to know the nature of the prior contact.

Gleason and I hadn't been working publicly with the flag for very long when we met McKissick at a rally in Elizabeth. He was, at that time, national director of CORE and this was a local chapter-sponsored rally. A friend of ours, a member of the choir at my church, was in charge of the meeting. Arthur was one of the more active residents of the community, sometimes running rallies as though he were a one-man show, but always urging people to take a stance, to show support, to get involved in the civil rights crises of the times. Arthur had read the articles about the flag and wanted us there to make a brief presentation prior to McKissick's speech.

We got to church early. Arthur met us as we approached the pulpit and told us McKissick was in the minister's study. He wanted to take us back there to introduce us. There wasn't much light in the study but enough to see that McKissick was tired. We hated to impose on the few minutes of respite he was taking, but Arthur insisted that we use the opportunity to show the flag privately. McKissick said that he had heard about the flag and wanted to see it. We opened it, Arthur and Gleason holding it out while I talked about it. When I finished, he slumped back in his chair, his tiredness overtaking his interest and he asked in an expressionless voice whether we had approached any national organizations with it yet. Gleason told him no, that we would welcome any public support from CORE or from him. I added that we had been going piecemeal with the flag up to that point and that if he would say something favorable about it that night it would help. When we finished our separate pleas for his support, McKissick looked at the flag without saying a word for a long moment. When he spoke again he asked whether we had approached national CORE with the concept. We responded once more that we hadn't, that we were on the verge of trying to make contact with all of the organizations, hoping that the flag would serve as an umbrella for everyone, not just one group. We made it clear again that we welcomed any support he would give.

When he asked no more questions we realized that his tiredness was so overwhelming that we ought to give him his few minutes alone before he had to speak to the gathering audience. We thanked him again and withdrew from the study leaving him in the dim light to collect his energies and thoughts for the evening ahead. We left Arthur in the study with him and went out front to get ourselves ready for our presentation.

We had time to look over the audience and we were pleased to see many familiar faces there. People were buzzing, waiting not too patiently for the program to begin. While we waved to a few friends, we were concentrating on choosing the best spot to put the pole and its stanchion so that when photographs were made later of McKissick, the flag would be just to the rear and in plain view of the camera. By the time we got it set, Arthur, McKissick, and the obligatory ministers were coming out to their seats on the platform.

The eldest of the ministers rose and prayed enough to make electric bolts shoot from the sky and then after calling the blessings of God on the assembly and its purpose for gathering, he really shot a bolt for us when he asked for "... the rays of God's sunshine to fall on the flag and let it shine as a beacon for all the children caught in the blackest night of torment in our troubled times." It was even more singular when Arthur introduced me as a homeboy he knew well, and had known since a little boy singing in the choir. Arthur was emphatic in reiterating the Reverend's prayer for the success of the flag.

I was nervous making this presentation. Gleason and I had been through only a few weeks of public meetings since the first news article had appeared, but this was the first time we had been in front of an audience with so many familiar faces in it. The audience was receptive through and it seemed that there were feelings of good wishes among them that made it easier to plow through the presentation. As I neared the end of the little speech, Gleason came over to the flag and held it out with a flourish. The audience responded with a tremendous applause. It was a good moment for each of us.

When McKissick moved up to give his speech, we settled in the front row to give our full attention to him. He was remarkable. The tiredness we had seen only a short while earlier had vanished; his voice was sure and controlled and his shoulders back. He gave every appearance of being rested, vigorous, glad to be in that little church in Elizabeth talking about the civil rights struggle and what CORE was doing. As we listened, I realized that the man exemplified some important characteristics; self-discipline that was the source of energy when needed, and a sense that supreme effort would and could be made when the occasion required it. Only his rumpled shirt betrayed the miles he had covered in that day. He gave the flag a plug, a few words of support for a concept that he though had merit. His words were carefully chosen, the words a consummate politician would use when in strange territory, not knowing how much power was wielded by the men who had held out the flag to a hometown audience and been given more than a generous applause. If we had been in North Carolina making a speech on his stamping grounds, we would have tried to make the same kind of careful remarks, enough to leave the audience with the sense that there was some tie, some connection, some bond between ourselves and the host.

When he finished his speech and sat down, it was evident once more that his sixteen-hour day had bested him, that he was near exhaustion. Luckily the meeting ended soon after and we had a chance to get close enough for a final handshake. He said he had still another speech to make elsewhere and wished us luck with the flag.

It was McKissick's recognition of the flag that was my last comment to Jake and the group. If he had any recollection of that meeting in Elizabeth there was perhaps some initial ground already broken that might make it easier for him to agree to see us.

Jake was eager to move on that possibility and for days I called him hoping to hear that contact had been made. It took a while but word came that McKissick would be in town and that he would discuss the flag with the group.

Joe, Ted and I were there waiting on the afternoon that Jake had promised McKissick would arrive. While we waited we went through all the possible responses he might give once my presentation was finished. Joe was a one-man cheering squad as he recounted how many people had become involved and that this was just one more run-through that would be equally successful. Securing the support of a nationally known figure was going to make the difference.

"I hope he remembers that time we met before." The words slipped out. It wasn't my usual style to share that kind of inner worry with Joe or Ted, but it was out.

"Think positively, Mel. He'll remember."

And he did. When McKissick arrived with an associate of his, he shook my hand with a comment that indicated his recollection of that church and our talk.

McKissick's friend took a seat near the window. He had been introduced as an economic analyst, part of the entourage of supporters who were planning Soul City. Pete was young and silent; he sat through the meeting without opening his mouth. His role that day was never clear to any of us.

Joe made a couple of opening remarks then gave me the floor to make my pitch. Once more the familiar words started to flow. Everybody in the room had heard it except McKissick and Pete. We were, therefore, totally unprepared when it became apparent that Floyd McKissick had silently slipped into a deep sleep. I couldn't have been talking more than three minutes when the sound of deep breathing overtook my description of the symbols on the flag.

I kept going, looking toward the unknown Pete as my primary listener, hoping that somehow McKissick would awaken without our having to shake him out of his slumber. After a catnap of about five minutes, he awoke, looked at the group, and pulled himself upright in his chair. "I'm tired. Been doing a lot of traveling working with Soul City." He make no apology for sleeping; instead he went right into a statement that must have been prepared no matter what had been the contents of my presentation. He said that if we needed the use of his name we had it and he would be part of the project!

That was it. He made no mention of setting up contracts, arranging media coverage, opening doors to organizations or any of the things we had hoped he would offer. I listened to him and realized that my reactions were mixed. Floyd McKissick was offering the use of his name; that was good. He was offering nothing else; that was not. Maybe Jake had not communicated fully what we thought we had made clear --- that we needed a point man, someone who could weld together by force of his connections and public recognition, a means to more actively promote the flag. We needed active support and, to be truthful, active leadership to get us beyond production.

His willingness to participate and the use of his name and no other commitment was a start though and we expressed our appreciation. We stood to shake hands and take a few pictures, and then he was gone, taking silent Pete with him.

As the door closed behind them, Joe and Ted sank into their chairs. I stood at the window shaking my head in amazement. Behind me Ted was saying, "This guy might be interested but he was sleeping. Sleeping!" My comment that we really didn't know how interested he was since he seemed so busy that he couldn't work actively with us, fell into a silence in the room. Joe came back with, "He wouldn't have committed himself to any-thing if he wasn't interested and didn't have the time to give to it."

That consoling though held me over to the next day. Jake told me we would meet at his office in early October, a couple of weeks away.

The entire group gathered that day. There was an air of expectation as we shook hands around and grouped ourselves so that McKissick was the focal point.

He opened up immediately with the thought that we ought to wait until after Christmas to get into any intense planning or activity. He made good sense when he remarked that a dilution of effort would follow if we attempted to crash into public view against the general preoccupation with the season. Considering that the manufacturers had not yet produced anything but sample runs and there was nothing to go to market with, his statement was on target. Somebody in the group mentioned the possible need for a marketing study with the sample runs. We tossed the idea around for a few minutes finally rejecting it when Ted said that the manufacturers had more than enough distribution points nationwide to meet the demands for promotional goods once exposure was given to the flag by McKissick.

At that point McKissick said he wanted careful consideration given to an idea he had. He looked at me warily. He wanted a name change --- from Black American Flag to Black American Heritage Flag. His words were met with silence; everybody sat there looking first at him then at me, waiting to hear my response. I asked why he thought the change necessary. While there were no qualms about the word *heritage*, it was most important to me to know why he wanted that word included. He responded only that he thought people would consider it important, that it carried a connotation with it that would be helpful when we turned to full promotion. The group chewed on the word for a few minutes, nobody saying that the change would be negative, somebody venturing that it could lend even greater dignity to the flag. I agreed with that but asked that they let me sleep on it, let me deal privately with any transformation of the concept. They agreed to give me the time realizing the depth of my feelings about preserving the flag as originally designed.

The discussion turned. Joe had a different concern: Ways would have to be found to provide meeting time for McKissick and myself so that we could focus on the philosophical base of the flag in preparation for its promotion. He was concerned that there would be total understanding and agreement between us to prevent any public fracture later. Everybody knew I was working nights and that day hours needed to be arranged for both McKissick and me. It was not easy to settle on times that were convenient to both of us and we realized that we would have to meet catch-as-catch-can for a while.

The meeting ended on an upbeat note. Things rested on my dealing with the name change, and we had been able to arrange a convenient time for everyone to come together again a few days later.

It took me less that an hour to locate Lee in California and bring him up to date. He caught the exhilaration in my voice. He was pleased to hear me report that McKissick had agreed to work with us, that the group felt it had accomplished something that morning, that I was going to accept the suggested name change. It was then that I realized he had his own channels for keeping contact with the project. He told me that the manufacturers were ready to put up big money to promote the flag and that they wanted an extended period on the contract. The first six months had nearly ended and the men were anxious to negotiate an extension. He advised me to grant the extension for another six months and give them first refusal for another year. Lee's advice had always been good and I took it this time.

The next session with McKissick was scheduled for a few days prior to Thanksgiving but he was unable to attend. Nonetheless the group met with Jake to review progress made on developing ideas for discussion, ideas related to using McKissick's name to get a promotion campaign underway. Jake apologized for McKissick's absence then dropped a bomb on us. McKissick wanted another change. He wanted some part of the flag to be changed to include the color green.

"Why?" I asked.

"For Africa."

"We're working with a flag for Black Americans that is supposed to represent them. The flag already has symbols on it that had their roots in Africa so why do we need to change the colors?"

Jake answered calmly, "Floyd brought up the question and I'm simply transmitting it to you."

"I'm not interested in changing. I don't want to change it."

The anger boiled in me at the thought of another change. Ted urged me to think about it, to not make a hasty decision on the spot.

"At least take overnight to consider this, Mel. You dealt with the name change after some thought. Give yourself and the flag the same time to consider this possibility."

Indignation was still flaring in me as I told him that green marked the Irish, that long ago I had explored hundreds of books seeking a common denominator among flags representing African nations and that I knew green was not that denominator. Again my question rose, "Why the color green? Why can't it stay the way Gleason and I designed it? Why make this change? Why even ask it?"

Ted tried again to soothe me, to urge me to sleep on it, take as long as needed to reach a calm decision about it.

He was right; maybe I had overreacted and needed to get away from the group to give this the consideration that was being asked. They knew it would have to be my decision and they were willing to wait.

As we left Jake's office, Joe invited me to stop back downtown at his place for some coffee. When I got there he was waiting, radiating his characteristic serenity. He poured coffee for me and sank into his big chair. He wanted to talk and it was plain that he would deal with the color change. I trusted Joe and knew that he would not mislead me when he finally got around to saying whatever was on his mind. When he did open up, it was a quiet conversation between friends about something that concerned them both. He asked how I felt about making the change.

"I don't see any reason for it."

"I'm with you. I don't see any reason either. You changed the name and we agreed with you that it was positive change that couldn't possibly hurt either the flag's past or its future. But this is different."

"It sure is different. I'm not happy with even the suggestion of a change as big as this. I just can't understand why it even came up."

"Not important, Mel. What matters is what you're going to do about the suggestion."

Joe was wrong. This particular change that McKissick was suggesting was important and it was critical to understand the reason behind the suggestion.

I knew that there were segments of the black population that were beginning to show a red, black, and green banner, that on some college campuses pseudo-fraternal organizations with esoteric names had adopted banners that used those three colors. But the issue remained as to whether McKissick was riding the tide of this emerging nationalistic representation or whether he had some other reason for making the suggestion. There seemed no point in discussing that with Joe so I rode along with his last comment and told him that it required some thinking on my part, that it would be given consideration but that, at this point, it was likely there would be no change.

Joe was comfortable with that response, reminding me that he and the others had samples ready in the flag's colors but could make changes if necessary. It would all depend on my decision.

I left his office not long after that, anxious to get off by myself to come to terms with this challenge. This was going to take longer than overnight to settle; too much time and energy had been spent with the flag as it had been designed to make a change on a whim even though there was the promise of assistance in promoting the flag. How much value did the assistance have when weighed against the intrinsic worth of the colors in the original design? Was the change suggested as a not-too-subtle means of making the flag over so that it would become someone else's creation? How much did it matter that samples had already been prepared in red, black and gold? Was it a dilution of the flag to change it? Would the concept be strengthened if the growing popularity of a red, black and green banner springing up in places around the country were absorbed into this flag? Would it appear that it was more important to ride along with those colors than it was to maintain the integrity of the flag as designed? Would the flag indeed be compromised, if the change were made? Could I tolerate even the idea of compromising this thing to which so much of my life had been devoted?

It is difficult to explain the thought processes that one goes through in trying to resolve a problem like this. It required more time than expected to try to unravel all the ends that always led back to the most critical question--would the flag be what it was if this change were made? The answer always came immediately: an emphatic NO! For good or ill, retaining all that the flag was designed to convey was the charge I placed before myself.

It took nearly two weeks to deal with the questions and to know in my innermost self that I could live with the consequences, whatever they might be. I decided to make no change. During those weeks, the group and I met several times reviewing samples, talking about things related to the new contract. Nobody pressured me for my decision on the colors. Day by day it became more certain that there would be no clarification from McKissick as to why he wanted green in the flag. By late December the resolve to not subvert the flag through any change was firm though the decision was not conveyed to the group for a few days more.

In the meantime Joe called to make an offer that radically altered my life for the next year. He suggested that I come on board as a full-time paid consultant to work with BLAM. The group was anxious to have my time fully and they were ready to pay for it. It would mean that I could give up the crazy hours and the miles of driving back and forth from Jersey each day, ending the snatched sleep and anxieties about steady income to support my family. Joe nailed down the offer with the comment that my time was already committed to the project and since I was, in effect, the catalyst for any movement that might occur, I might as well be paid for the time spent.

It was a hard offer to refuse, but time was needed to think about it and to discuss it with my wife, so I begged off an immediate answer, promising to let him know as soon as possible.

She and I talked that evening. She was concerned still about the time being given to the flag, perceiving it as a tilting at windmills that would never blow a favorable wind my way. She was not happy with the hours I was keeping; meals were uncertain, family matters given short shrift as the time to deal with them was squeezed between naps and the need to prepare for the free-lance display jobs. She wondered whether going full time with the flag would make a difference, whether all of this was really so important that I could let slide the things that a family was supposed to be doing and impose on her and our daughter my obsession with the flag and all that came with that overwhelming devotion to an idea.

Her arguments had validity. She was a victim of this obsession even though it had not been intended that neither, she nor our daughter should suffer for anything from me --time, money or companionship. My marriage was important to me, my role as a parent equally so. It didn't make me feel any too much a man when I could see our friends and neighbors acquiring worldly goods that were not easy for us to get given the circumstances. I thought about trying to tell her once again what the flag meant to me and decided against it. She knew already. She was pragmatic in this situation; I, the idealist. I asked her understanding while the transition was made to full-time work with the project, promising that somehow time would be found to be more a part of the family, more attuned to their needs. Again she acquiesced, recognizing that my determination to give this try was firm, that there had to be the chance to find out once and for all whether concentrated effort would create a real future for the flag. We both remembered that I had asked her to give me until the end of 1971 and she had agreed. Now we were approaching the beginning of 1972 and she was being asked again to give me time.

"Just a year," I asked of her. "One year."

"Don't do it," Lee said the next day when I called to try it out on him. "These men have not done enough in the promotion end of the contract to warrant your taking that kind of flyer right now. Hold off for a while and see what happens in the planning for publicity."

That set me back. I had been so focused on the possibility of having, for once, twenty-four hours a day to give to the project, that no consideration had been given to how the time would be spent. Lee's cool assessment raised a point that had not surfaced in my talk with my wife. He was right, of course; it was not enough to have time at your disposal, it was vital to have a feasible plan for the use of that time.

Joe asked often over the next couple of weeks whether I had decided to come on board. Each time he raised the question I ducked it, telling him of my need to get through the Christmas season, completing some free-lance jobs and taking some time with my family. He'd have an answer by the new year. He was content with my responses. He knew that, no matter what, I'd take the offer even though it hadn't been said.

Shortly after Christmas I spoke with Lee again, giving him my thinking about the importance to me personally having one good shot at the promotion of the flag even if there were no firm plan for that promotion.

He asked whether I had made up my mind about the flag's colors.

"Yes, I have. There will be no change."

He asked whether I had weighed what he said in our last talk. Again the response was "Yes."

Finally, he said, "Well, I guess you have to do it. You've been around with the flag for years and you know in what direction it should go. Maybe the support of McKissick and Joe and the rest is enough for you to develop a sound plan for promotion and make it a go. Good luck with it and stay in touch."

Two days before the end of the year I called Joe to tell him that I would be there to work full-time.

"Great, Mel. This is going to do it. Look for you Monday."

January was a blur of activity. Settling into space at Joe's office, getting listings of people to contact from every possible source, developing mailings, yanking small flags off the manufacturers' benches to go in the mailings, setting up a post office box, meeting with the group at their offices to review the samples that were now ready for full-scale production turned the month into a whirlwind. My calendar was jammed with appointments with the manufacturers who responded quickly to the instant access and the new pressures that my constant presence seemed to place on production.

Late in the month an appointment was made to stop by Jake's office. My decision about not using green in the flag had not yet been shared, nor had we heard from Jake or McKissick while that decision was in abeyance. It was time to settle this one.

When I arrived, Jake and an assistant of his, a young black man who had sat in on one or two meetings, were waiting. Almost before I could sit down Jake wanted to know what the decision was. When I told him that the colors would stay as they were, the assistant, who had been standing at the window taking in the sights of the city below, said without turning around, "Make the change."

I looked at his back, absorbing the implicit command and knowing that a refusal to change my mind would have an impact that might be regretted later.

"No, no change!"

Jake got up, effectively ending the meeting.

"If that's it, we'll have to go along with you. I'll let Floyd know your decision."

Two days later Jake called. Floyd McKissick would not work with the flag if there were no color change. If Floyd would not work with the flag, neither would he.

His words were not totally unexpected. It had been taking a chance to say no to the change and the refusal to go along had been made with the certainty that somebody would bow out. It was not expected that Jake would go out with McKissick, but so be it. My hopes that he would stay with us and try the avenue of Charles Evers' interest in the project, went out too with his words. I thanked him for his time and told him we would move ahead.

"And, thank McKissick for me for the time he gave to it."

Joe was nearby as the call was completed. He wanted to know what had been said and was ready to convene the group to hear it. In short order everyone was there, anxiety showing on their faces. Someone asked whether the ramifications of refusing to go along with the change had been considered fully. I told him that they had, that the flag as originally designed was more important than one man's opinion about the colors it should display and that I was prepared to bear the aftermath of that decision. I reminded them that we had no real plan for promotion so how could the loss of Lamarr and McKissick seriously affect the situation?

We were right where we had been in terms of getting together a feasible plan for promotion -- nowhere. All we had achieved in the few months of association with McKissick was a new name for the flag and that was it.

We still needed that one missing link vital to any progress from that point. We needed a publicity man who could pull it all together for us. We had a product and a potential market and no plan to develop a demand for the product.

Chapter 12

W e were still on square one and the place was getting crowded! The men finally understood what I had been saying for months -- get a public relations man! At last there was consensus that I was right. Where should we look for someone? No answers. Everybody would have to cast around and run a few contacts to ground until the need was met.

Impatience took over; there was no way to sit around and wait for BLAM to provide leads to a public relations person. I got to work on it the next day. A friend suggested that a talk with a young black magazine publisher might be productive. A telephone call to the publisher netted an appointment for the next week. The meeting was virtually worthless. When I laid out the project he showed great disinterest, this perhaps stemming from his need to get himself and his magazine firmly established and not needing to be compromised by any association with the flag. When pressed for some lead to anyone he knew he finally suggested a name. He even placed a call and set an appointment for the following Tuesday in the man's office. I thanked him for his time and the lead and wished him well with his magazine.

On Tuesday, promptly at 1:30, I stood in the man's office and knew I was in the wrong church and wrong pew. He was stoned out of his head, nodding before I could reach over to give him a handshake. He never even heard me say my name.

When I got back to Joe's office, the group had gathered like bridesmaids waiting for the processional music to begin. It was impossible to tell them that one more young black man had bitten the dust, succumbed to the lure of a high and gone off to his private dreamland. I told them he must have had a heavy martini lunch and that he just wasn't in condition to communicate clearly. They bought it.

They were an unusual collection of men, somehow sharing the quality of being able to empathize with my dreams about the flag while maintaining a sure footing in the arena where they existed -- the production of goods. they were floundering along with me in trying to find the right path to get the goods out to a market everyone knew existed, but nobody had a key to unlocking. They may have felt helpless in a way, knowing that they could meet a demand for goods but not being able to produce a clamor for the products. They always managed somehow to find the words to keep up my spirits, encouraging me as door after door was tried, offering solace when one then another lead went nowhere.

February proved to be a turning point. It began with letters, responses from some of the leading black figures of the day, and built up daily as my calendar filled with more and more appointments.

The letters were a mixed bag, some powerful in their encouragement and others, pale echoes of responses received years earlier.

Augustus Hawkins' letter, the first of several from Congressmen, boosted the sagging spirits of every man in the group. Hawkins sent his thanks for the enclosures accompanying my letter and offered his assistance with the words,"... do not hesitate to call on me." This was the first open response that wasn't hedging, and it was followed in rapid succession by others from Congressmen to whom the January mailing had been directed.

A couple of years earlier, Edward Brooke had written his regrets, denying an endorsement of the flag because of its possible nationalistic sentiments. Now he wrote to thank me for the small banner and pin and to say that he was "... pleased to learn the symbol and the ideas behind it, (are) receiving such wide acceptance...". He wished me every success in my "... most worthy efforts."

Before February ended, there were responses from Charles Rangel, George Collins and Charles Diggs. Rangel wished me continued success in the effort to "... gain organizational support of this project ...," while Collins reviewed a bill he had co-sponsored to "... improve the opportunity for students in educational facilities to study cultural heritage of the various ethnic groups in the nation." Diggs wrote that he had displayed the flag in his office. That was something! Joe and the others were in seventh heaven when they read that letter. We shared a common sense of accomplishment to learn that somewhere in the hallowed halls of the Capitol there was a Black American Heritage Flag in plain view in a Congressman's office.

The feeling that things were beginning to move led to more active involvement on the part of the men in getting me out to meet with other manufacturers.

One day in mid-February, Joe suggested that a friend of his in the record business might provide some help. Delite Records was promoting and up-and-coming group -- Kool and the Gang -- and the representative from the company who met with us thought there might be a way to fit the flag into their promotion of the rock group. We gave him a batch of lapel pins as the session ended and shook hands on his word to get back to us soon.

A few days later, he did come back, bringing with him the weirdest idea that had surfaced to date. He had given the lapel pins to the members of Kool and the Gang. They had worn them on a road engagement and gotten very positive reactions to their answers to queries about the meaning of the pins. The man from the record company thought we could build on that beginning and send me on tour with the musicians, The point to my going was that somewhere in each performance I would be introduced as "Mr. Black America," dressed in a cape made from the flag design. He guaranteed instant recognition and coverage of a presentation featuring an appearance like that. What did we think of the idea?

"It's trash. I'll have no part of that."

That ended that contact.

A few days later, another record company was brought into the picture by Joe. This one pushed black artists and had some very young, very businesslike, competent men who came to talk with us. As usual, there were the preliminary concept-selling words before we could broach the topic of what the one hand could do for the other. This session ended with the customary "We'll get back to you later," but there was a sense that the men from this company were interested and might offer something of substance.

In our second meeting they made no offers of help directly, but did say that they had discussed the idea with a friend in Newark. We asked who, one answered, "A prominent black nationalist leader." The "friend" was a vice-president of the record company, working closely with white owners as black artists were being pushed more and more through the company.

I put that piece of information away in the back of my mind knowing that if there were a prominent black nationalist leader connected with the record company this would probably be our last meeting and I would not get the chance again to lay out an idea that had been brewing since our first contact with them. I wanted to see what their reactions would be to the idea of putting the flag somewhere on the cover of an album or two of a rising black musician. It would involve little in effort on anybody's part. The men were interested but once again pushed off with "Later, we'll get back to you."

They disappeared as expected. We could only surmise that when they reported back to the company, somebody had put the stamp of disapproval on any relationship with the flag. I took it personally, seeing a bitter reminder that black leaders, nationalist or not, did not react favorably to the flag. It reminded me of a particularly painful encounter with a black leader in a public meeting. It had been in 1968 and the "leader" had been LeRoi Jones.

The United Brothers, a mostly local group of young men in Newark, had invited Gleason and me to make a presentation of the flag at the beginning of one of their public meetings. Gleason had had to fulfill another engagement that night and John, the public relations man then working with us, had gone with me. He pointed out faces in the audience, including Kenneth Gibson, soon to be elected the first black mayor of Newark. The United Brothers were working furiously throughout the city to mobilize potential black voters, getting them registered and priming them to exercise this right of citizenship. The meeting was one more in a series of public forums to which speakers were invited to intensify public consciousness of this right and responsibility as well as to articulate the premises on which the United Brothers made their stand.

Ron Karenga and LeRoi Jones were the featured speakers for the evening's program. I felt honored to have been invited to the same platform on which speakers of such note were to be present. Karenga and Jones had not yet arrived and so they didn't hear me begin the ten-minute presentation.

Chairman Harry Wheeler's introduction had been forthright. He said, "Some people have dreams, others create dreams. This man created a dream down the road in Linden and he's here to speak about unity among our people, the same unity the United Brothers want to develop among us."

The invitation to speak had rested on the strength of the newspaper coverage of the unfurling of the flag in Newark in early March of '68. There were some in the audience who had not heard of the flag. When I was introduced, applause was scattered. I recognized a few faces. It was a chance, however , to make the presentation that I hoped would focus their attention on the possibilities of a common rallying point - the flag.

As I began to talk, the shape and form of the speech flowed from the news coverage of the flag's unfurling, with emphasis on the fact that, in Newark, recognition had been given that could not be secured in my own hometown. All praise Newark! The mood created with those words and the attention of the audience was palpable as I moved into explaining what the symbols on the flag represented. Just then, a note was placed on the lectern by Wheeler, telling me to take ten minutes more. That was a pleasure, the opportunity to talk about the need for pride, responsibility, identity, discipline and effort. We perceived these to be inherent in what the flag represented. I was deep into talking when Karenga and Jones headed down the left-hand aisle, on their way backstage. That was the clear signal to wind down my remarks. My final words, spoken as Karenga and Jones passed through the doors to the stage , were that, "... people had heard of the great philosophers - Plato, Aristotle, Socrates, even the words of the world's greatest playwright, Shakespeare, but I want you to know of a great black philosopher, a singing philosopher - Ray Charles. He's told us, 'Mama may have, Papa may have, but God bless the child who has his own'. And , we have our own. We, in Black America, have our own flag".

The audience erupted with tremendous applause behind those words just as Jones arrived behind the curtains at the side of the stage. As I passed by him and the coterie of followers standing nearby, I heard one man say to Wheeler, "Whoever put him on the program is to know that we don't want him on any more programs for the brothers. Jones doesn't want him here."

The words penetrated the applause, shooting a large hole in the good sounds the audience was making. The words were disturbing, foolish, back-biting words that reflected the poor state of unity among black people, evident in the fractured efforts of our so-called leaders. If my words had validity and the audience understood the cry for a coming together, why should it pose such a threat to Jones? I had been invited to speak about the flag and that's what I had done. There had been no denigration of Jones or the United Brothers or their purposes or programs. It had seemed to me that what had been said was as supportive of them as it was promotional for the flag. Hie attitude was startling, unpleasant, and unexpected.

The lesson learned from this encounter was a bitter one. Generalized Black leaders seemed so fearful of losing their grasp on the minds of their followers, they could brook nothing that looked like competition. If the black nationalist leader who had connections with the record company reacted typically, he turned thumbs-down on the proposal to promote the flag, practicing the same put-down that was verbalized at Jones' direction. It was more pathetic as typical of black leaders, but that's the way it was.

After the record company disappeared, things simmered down to a slow crawl. It was becoming more and more apparent to me that without someone on the payroll to plan and direct a concerted effort to get publicity we were going exactly nowhere. Once more I asked the men to help me find the public relations man that the project needed. Without such a person there was little point in my continuing to work with them.

Three weeks later, in mid-February 1972, Joe found Bill Tappin, a professional public relations man then working for several companies in New York.

A preliminary meeting took place between Joe and Tappin before his name was mentioned to me, the same kind of preliminaries that always took place before the session at which I was expected to sell the concept. At least that kind of "feeling out" occurred before I had contact and it is likely that members of the group had tried many sources and had been turned down once the flag was described with the word "black". Someone let it slip once that while I thought they were sitting on their hands and refusing to search for a PR man, they were in fact at work, meeting negative attitudes on every side. Bill Tappin had shown an open mind about the project and was willing to go into exploratory discussion.

He read the articles, brochures, listened to my spiel, concentrated on what we thought we needed from him. He was still interested as this ground was covered; he was willing to work for us, not as a member of BLAM Associates, but rather as an employee. His function: to plan and implement a publicity campaign that would provide a positive kick-off for the flag.

This was it! We finally had someone competent at public relations committed to the project work. Everything revved up from that day. There were not enough hours to get everything completed that seemed so important to getting the campaign off the ground.

It was essential first that Bill understand the philosophy that we wanted the campaign to exemplify. It was important that the campaign be conducted to secure positive and favorable publicity that was to as large an audience as possible. It was imperative that the presentation of the flag to the public would not disrespect or derogate the national flag in any way. Dignity and grace had to be the hallmarks of the campaign. It had to be kicked-off in New York, for obvious reasons, with as much national media attention as possible. If no organizations would lend their names to the campaign, then we would start at scratch and organize a program that would get the attention to the flag and what it represented.

Bill spent hours with me discussing the flag as a concept. Pride, responsibility, identity, discipline, and effort were the descriptors for the campaign we were undertaking. If what the flag represented was not demonstrated in the promotion, there was no point in even trying.

Bill listened intently, absorbing every word, nodding his head in agreement and understanding. He was anxious to be off and running. To prove that he understood the desire to have organizational support, if possible, he set up a luncheon meeting with the Chief Counsel for the NAACP - Julius Williams.

We met Williams at Downey's Pub for a fascinating hour in which Bill talked excitedly about the flag. He pushed for an appointment to see Roy Wilkins, with the intent of exploring the organization's interest in the merits of the flag. Williams, affable and non-committal, expressed only his personal interest in learning more about the flag. He took a lapel pin and asked what other kinds of promotional items were available. We talked about BLAM and it's relationship to the campaign and covered as much of the early history of the flag as time permitted. At the end Williams gave me his telephone number and asked that I call him in a few days.

Later at the office, I packaged a flag and the usual items that went in a mailing, hoping that this would be a break in the pattern of disinterest that had been set long ago. Once again the memories of those Sundays at NAACP meetings at Liberty Baptist Church flooded my mind. The speakers who had come to talk about making contributions to the race and who had talked about pride in self and people were almost standing in front of me. I could see my mother beaming as our little songs and recitations opened those meetings and then her watchful eye on us as we sat through the speeches. We had listened and accepted the charge to do something worthwhile with our lives and this was it, my contribution to the progress of black people.

I waited a couple of days after the package was delivered, trying to give Williams time to review the contents and do whatever he could to get entree to Wilkins for me. When I made my first call to his office he said he had not yet had time to talk about the flag with anyone. "Call again." Several calls later, it finally dawned on me that this was a dead-end. Secretaries answered with - "Mr. Williams is in conference." There was no request to call back. I didn't.

It would not pay to dwell on lack of success with getting entree to the NAACP; it was more important to use the time to advantage to push on as many fronts as possible. Bill's first attempt to set up viable contacts hadn't panned out, but he was turning to other avenues. My personal efforts to find assistance were continuing at the same double-time pace.

Letter-writing proceeded; names appearing in black publications were distant and unknown but still represented a possibility for broadening awareness if not outright endorsement. A book shelf in my office filled with those publications as the secretary was kept busy sending out letter after letter. When newspapers announced visits to New York by prominent black personalities, I tried to make contact by phone. I pushed as hard and fast as possible to find a willing ear.

Bill called daily as he pursued one contact after another, trying to find a "hook," as he called it. He made suggestions as idea after idea popped into his head, suggestions that were rejected as too flamboyant or too narrow. We went through several of the more plausible ideas, exploring each in detail for its merits. He spent hours every day talking with a huge assortment of agents, promoters, advertisers, managers and anyone else he could buttonhole. One of his contacts mentioned a group of black youngsters in Pittsburgh who were exceptional musicians. Bill got as much information as he could about the group and began to weave together the fabric of a campaign that would absorb us totally over the next six weeks.

He came in with a barebones sketch of a plan featuring the child-musicians soon after the non-productive meeting with the NAACP Chief Counsel. The plan was to bring the children to New York to perform somewhere in the city, providing the drawing card to focus media attention on the flag. He had no details as he sketched the outline of the plan but he thought it possible to spread the appearances of the children over several days with presentations of the flag to prominent black figures and city officials and to do it all with dignity and grace. He went through the outline of these possibilities smoothly and quickly, generating enthusiasm within the group as he talked. We were pleased to see that Bill was producing something, that there was at least the shadowy outline of a proposal that could be worked on and made to become viable. This was real forward movement.

We wanted to know who the children were. Bill said that all he knew about them was that the all-black group of children had been taught to play the violin by a Catholic nun. The group, known as the Ozanam Strings, was well known and highly regarded in Pittsburgh. The forty-some well-disciplined children in the group were not yet proficient on the instrument, but apparently far enough along in their development to warrant exploring their potential for performances in New York.

Bill had not heard them personally, yet he told us enthusiastically that a campaign featuring black children performing classical music was the kind we wanted. He wanted a commitment from the group to explore the possibility of bringing the Strings to New York. If we began promptly to organize a campaign, taking as a given that the Strings measured up to their reputation, we might be able to bring them to New York in early April on their spring vacation from school.

We were interested? Yes! This one was worth following up. Bill was told to contact the director of the Strings and to begin to work out details of a two or three day visit to New York for the group.

We were committed! We poured every ounce of our energy into Bill's plan over the next six weeks. He was talking good stuff, active planning, movement. This was a far cry from someone suggesting that the flag be made into a cape and draped around my shoulders at a rock concert. It sounded good and Bill had sold us all.

In a few days Bill had arranged for two representatives of the Ozanam Strings to come to New York at BLAM's expense. He wanted exposure for the children and assurance that we would take as much concern for their welfare as for publicizing the flag. It was important that Pitts understood what the flag was about if he was to convey to the children its meaning. Those young people would have to be able to respond to questions about the flag as well as they would have to play their instruments.

Bill had assembled a preliminary promotion kit, a bag full of possible appearances and performances, some recreational activities, free time to tour the city, and meetings with public officials and maybe a sports figure or two. Everything was tentative but possible. Pitts and his associate were excited about the opportunity that was unfolding in front of them. The Ozanam Strings had earned recognition in their hometown but having the chance to try their wings in New York was magic. None of us dreamed that in only a couple more years the Strings would be invited to Japan to perform and would do so to great acclaim. This was here and now and Pitts was eager to hear more about the planning. Once it was established that the Strings could be in the city for four days, Bill jumped at the chance to extend the schedule of activities, always keeping uppermost the need to provide adequate time for rest, relaxation, and recreation for the youngsters along with the demanding performance schedule that would be required.

The discussion with Pitts and his associate ended with enthusiasm on both sides. He would return to Pittsburgh with a tentative schedule that was more than satisfactory where the children's welfare was concerned. We were pleased that we had his commitment that the Strings would come to New York and agreed that someone would make the trip to Pittsburgh shortly to hear them in a rehearsal.

Bill turned to us after the men left and said he had to leave to get to work firming up things. He was going to check into the possibility of performances at the Apollo Theatre and at the Port Authority Bus Terminal, recreational excursions in the city, maybe a trip to the United Nations building. He had to see which sports teams would be in town during that week in April and who he could get to make a personal appearance with the children. Ideas were tumbling out of him at breakneck speed; he was developing an agenda for a fantastic four days.

He left, promising us that this would be the kick-off to end all promotions. He had to get to work on the details that would make it a success, he said. "If I work on the details, all the big things will take care of themselves. It's going to work."

Joe was pleased with Bill. He had been the one to find Tappin and it was important to him personally that this work well. Bill and I met almost daily to review progress over the next weeks and each time Joe was waiting when I returned to the office, eager to hear the latest development, anxious to know what he could do to help. His supportive comments and objective assessments of plans as they developed were enough.

It was surprising to me that few contacts fell through as we moved through the next weeks. Bill, it was evident, was well-known and had a way of talking up an idea to make other people want to become involved. One avenue he developed for promoting both the coming appearance of the Strings and the flag involved me very directly.

He and I met for lunch one day at a very fashionable restaurant, one frequented by movie stars, theatre people, producers. The aura of the place fascinated me so that I was not really listening to Bill at first. Soon it dawned on me that he wanted me to appear on his radio show, a weekly program aired globally to the Armed Forces. He was saying that doing a piece about the flag would be a natural inasmuch as the *Stars and Stripes* had carried the earliest article about the flag way back in '67. He had my full attention as he set a date for the broadcast and told me where his studio was located in lower Manhattan. Nobody in that restaurant was as excited about their pursuits as I.

I arranged with my brother-in-law, an amateur photographer, to be at the studio to begin a photo history of the campaign that Bill was developing and began to prime myself for my first radio show.

The day arrived; I was at the studio early, well ahead of the time set for the broadcast. Bill was there bustling around his office for a while then settling into a relaxation routine that he needed before going on air. It would have been well if I had borrowed some of the relaxation process. Almost immediately after the broadcast began I froze! Bill asked leading questions; my answers came back in monosyllables. He sat there looking at me encouragingly as he posed questions. I sat there agreeing with everything he said, adding nothing to my "yes" or "no".

It was the longest ten minutes of my life and probably the most exhausting interview Bill had ever conducted. To cap it off, my brother-in-law never showed. Good thing too, as nobody needed visual reminders of a fiasco.

The experience taught me a lesson. When the interview ended I had a serious talk with myself about microphones and studio crews, unfamiliar settings, and preparation for a one-shot, no re-take situation in which I had to present an idea and to do it right the first time. What happened that day was never to happen again!

Bill was encouraging after the show, somehow finding words to ease my obvious pain over the way things had gone. Our relationship changed after that from a purely business basis to one marked by a quiet friendship and camaraderie as we moved through the rapidly developing stages of filling in the details of the campaign kit.

Sometimes in the meetings as ideas were presented and discussed, it seemed that there was a peculiar aloofness in the group leaving me in the middle of an invisible circle with everyone standing on the outer edge waiting for me to signal that things were all right. The manufacturers were there to produce a product that was to take off in many forms and move to the ends of the country, all from the effects of the promotional campaign that was being constructed. If that campaign fell apart or were unsuccessful, somebody would have to take the weight for its failure. If the failure were the result of negative publicity that could and should have been foreseen and avoided, it would be even worse. They were careful to let me make the critical decisions, determining whether some suggestion had merit, examining ideas for their potential worth, rejecting those that were demeaning in any way. It became lonesome in the middle of that circle surrounded by a group of white men working to develop a campaign to promote a flag that represented black pride. Lonesomeness had its virtues - one could feel a certain sense of authority in decision-making, but at least when Gleason was alive there was always someone to bounce thoughts to and get a response that came from common understanding and feeling about what black pride was.

Joe, with his usual empathy for people, had recognized the existence of that isolated spot in the middle of the circle. He must have been on the lookout for someone who could join the group in a capacity entirely different from that which each man now filled. He found that someone purely by chance at an advertisers' show in New York, a powerhouse of a woman, tall, black, stately, articulate. Mabel Morton, a regional sales manager for Johnson Products, did a lot of traveling for her company but she listened to Joe intently at the show and decided that she could find the time to come to a meeting.

Mabel came through the door of Joe's office, eyes glowing, soft voice reaching out, warmth and intelligence in every word and move. I knew when we met that she was going to be that listening post that was sorely missed, that comrade-in-blood who would give me the balancing weight as the tight-rope of decisions was walked. She never failed in that capacity.

Our first meeting was a tremendous boost to me. Joe was pleased that he had figured the chemistry right. She left that meeting with a firm promise to work on the project. Everything seemed to be falling into place. We were on the move. Literally.

Within a few days of his initial proposal of the plan, Bill came up with a complete presentation, synthesizing all the acceptable ideas, and firming the agenda for the Strings four-day visit. Mabel was impressed by what she heard, agreeing that it provided a positive springboard for the flag. When he wound up the presentation there was a huge smile on everybody's face. We had made tremendous headway, coming a long way past the disappointments of the dead-end meetings with all the contacts prior to Bill's coming on board. This man had brought something of substance to the project.

His plan was good: transportation, housing and meals would be paid for by BLAM with substantial discounts coming out of contacts Bill had made; there were affirmative responses from Percy Sutton's office: the Manhattten Borough President was pleased to meet with the children; the Liberian Ambassador was making his office available at the end of a tour of the United Nations Building and he himself would talk with the children. The Port Authority had given permission for a public performance using a mezzanine as the stage. Willis Reed would appear at a lunch at Madison Square Garden; reservations had been made with Circle Line for a morning's excursion and the crowning piece was the appearance at the Apollo Theatre. There were plans for publicity including arrangements for me to appear on the Joe Franklin television show. The only critical step that had to be taken now was for someone to go hear our prospective guest stars. That would have to be me. But before that, Bill thought it necessary to tie down the appearance at the Apollo so that when the trip to Pittsburgh was made, I could carry assurances of a firm agenda with me.

By the time Bill finished laying out the priorities for immediate action he had filled my calendar with appointments to meet Joe Franklin, Honi Coles at the Apollo and a tentative date to go to Pittsburgh. Each of these appointments had to be preceded by work lunches in which he would lay out the best approach to each of these essential meetings. Bill had seized the reins once assent was secured from the group. He was taking care of details in an admirable fashion, reminding us always that the big things would take care of themselves.

The meeting with Joe Franklin went well. I kept in mind the promise made to myself after the ruinous show with Bill and I was determined that, given the chance, the next appearance would be more satisfying to me personally. Joe Franklin was genial and cordial, exhibiting none of the ego-centered "star" qualities one might have expected from a man who was established in his own sphere. He put me at ease immediately. I looked forward to doing the show with little dread of my ability to project properly and effectively the message that had to be delivered. The meeting with Honi Coles got off to a shaky start but wound up just as smoothly.

Bill and I arrived at the Apollo right on time for our appointment only to find that Coles was not yet there. His assistant greeted us, listened while Bill presented the plan for the promotion with emphasis on the importance of an appearance at the home of the great black entertainers. The assistant was polite but told us it wouldn't work, that the week we had scheduled was the week that Nancy Wilson and Cannonball Adderley were appearing and he was certain that Mr. Coles would not like to rearrange anything with a top bill like that one. As he talked it turned out that what he really thought wouldn't work was our request to have the Strings appear before the usual opening time as a lead into the theatre's scheduled program. That would mean the assistant would have to come in early on that day and that was definitely not what he wanted to do.

We were about to give up when suddenly the door opened and Honi Coles moved gracefully, as only a life-long skilled dancer can, into the office. Bill beamed and rose to greet him, telling him how great he looked. Honi - tall, slim, elegantly dressed - was cordial. He seemed genuinely pleased to see Bill and that told me there was a real basis for the connection Bill had said he had with the Apollo. That was important; this whole campaign hinged on the fruitfulness of Bill's contacts and the greeting I had just seen augured well for all the other meetings we had scheduled with others important to filling in the details of the campaign.

Bill introduced me to Honi then set about describing what we wanted. He laid emphasis on the youth of the members of the Strings, the unique quality of performance they would bring to the Apollo and the boost that could be given to the flag if it were possible to make presentations to the guest stars already scheduled. Was it possible?

Honi replied, "We're to have Nancy and Cannonball as you know. I'd like to think you could do this, but you have to keep in mind that they won't perform until late in the evening and usually they don't come to the theatre until shortly before they go on stage. They may not be here for any presentation but I'll check it out for you. I'm making no promises now but give me a day or two and I'll let you know. It all depends on what their schedules are going to be and I'll have to check."

He wasn't saying no to anything! It was implicit that the appearance of the Strings was acceptable.

Honi Coles carried a lot of weight in that community. His position as manager of the Apollo extended into control of the block surrounding the theatre. A street type might rip off a passer-by somewhere further along that street but not near or in front of the Apollo. Honi was careful to maintain as strict control of the immediate environs as he did the programming that went inside. When he said he would get back to us by a certain time we could rely on his word.

On the way back to the office, Bill said again that it was necessary that I go to Pittsburgh soon to hear the Strings. Once again I was in the middle of the circle with my decision being the final one. The only thing that made me feel not too concerned about this decision was that my own experiences with music gave me some background to help judge the quality of performance and the strength of the youngsters to carry off one as important as this.

When Bill and I got back to the office, Joe and Ted were waiting to hear the results of our meeting with Coles. Bill asked me to tell it and it felt good to relay the comments and promises that had been made. Joe was elated. His stock in Bill was rising by the day as the pieces of the agenda fell into place. Somebody suggested that we go out for a drink to celebrate this stage of the plans and since it was late in the day anyhow, we found a quiet bar in the Village to make our toasts to success.

There were glasses raised in Bill's direction from all sides. He seemed to enjoy the plaudits for what had been accomplished so far, but as the evening wore on a certain kind of strain started to show. His shoulders slumped as we reviewed time and again the things that were in place and listed what had still to be done. It was an enormous undertaking and at that time only he fully realized just how big the thing was. His experience at promoting was far greater than any of us had and he knew that while I had to carry the weight of deciding that something would take place, he had the responsibility to see that it went according to schedule. He had to take care of the details and he well knew that a public relations man was only as good as his last performance. If things went well he could take the glory; if they failed, he would have to show how those he depended on failed to come through for him. That seemed an easy out for him but failure in any regard would seriously affect his "last performance." Bill was committed to the project; he had to produce. We were pleased that things were moving well but he was beginning to feel the weight of what had still to be put in place. He drank more than he should, probably, that night but held it well. Only the lines deepening in his face told of the growing strain he was under.

When I got home that night it was a pleasure to describe to my wife how things were going, to share with her the sense that a real campaign was developing and that it had merit, support, and excellent chances to produce the results we wanted. She was geniunely happy and somehow relieved that things were breaking well and we shared a good evening of hopeful talk about the coming success of the flag.

Two days later a call came from the owner of the restaurant in Madison Square Garden, confirming lunch reservations for the Strings, but with an unexpected turn that was even more exciting. The man knew that the Ozanam Strings was a Catholic-sponsored group and he had taken it on himself to advise the Brooklyn Diocese that they would be in town. He wondered whether it would be possible for the Strings to work in an additional performance at a church in Brooklyn? The answer was yes. That was an extra opportunity for exposure of both the Strings and the flag and we welcomed the bonus.

Bill was moving around town, plumping the event and meeting success at every turn. It was incredible that everything was popping at once and so positively. We were still in early March with a little less than a month to put all the final details into place. We knew that every minute would count as we moved toward the April 3rd kick-off date.

Things were moving on another front at the same time.

I had shared with Mabel the responses that had come from Washington in February. She read with interest the letter from Charles Diggs in particular, the one that said the flag was on display in his office. Shortly after that letter had arrived another came, this one from Dr. Charles Wesley, Executive Director of the Association for the Study of Negro Life and History. His response had been encouraging as he wrote, "This is a significant movement and has value for our thinking and reaction."

Those two letters had carried me into March adding lift to the good feelings that grew day by day as plans for the appearance of the Strings firmed up. Mabel thought we ought to go to Washington if for no other reason than to take a breather from the hectic pace that consumed our day and all our energy. But first she thought that it was worth it to make one more attempt to approach a major black organization for endorsement and she wanted me to try the Urban League this time. It seemed to us that with the solid planning we had in hand for a campaign that would result in good publicity, an organization need only give its endorsement to ride along at no cost to them. Mabel had no direct contact there, but thought a call to the public relations department might result in my getting to see someone. Neither of us could have guessed that the results would be far different from what we expected.

An appointment was made to see a Mr. Wilson whose role in the organization was not made clear in the telephone conversation but who was willing to sit down to hear what I had to say.

Mr. Wilson made it emphatically plain that the Urban League was not interested in the flag not even if it were offered to them as a fund-raiser. He let it be known that the organization was receiving grant monies from many sources and nobody there would have the time to pursue any further discussion of the flag in any form or for any purpose.

He seemed a little apologetic as he spoke, his voice softening as he made the statements that must have been the company line. My recovery from the rejection was slow in coming. Had he delivered his words with force or in haste, it would have been easy to pick up the portfolio, say thanks and get out of there. His apologetic demeanor, however, seemed to give a small opening so I plunged in and asked whether he knew anyone, anyone at all who might be able to help me accomplish the end I was after - recognition of the flag. He thought for a moment and then suggested that I contact black historians wherever they could be found, and one in particular, an Alton Davis, a man well-known in the Chicago and Boston areas a black historian with a large number of contacts. Dr. Davis might be a good person to reach, he thought.

I thanked Mr. Wilson and made my exit. In the lobby of the building I turned back to look at the directory which announced the Urban League's office and thought once more about the statements I had heard in my childhood, statements calling on black people to do something positive. What had those Sundays been for, what had those statements really meant if you approached the people who made those clarion calls and got not even the echo of a response from them when you went carrying your contribution in your hand?

Wilson had at least given me some leads, to Davis by name and to historians in general, scattered on black campuses North to South. For that I was grateful, but it was a bitter pill to swallow for the few moments that it took to get past the strong feeling of rejection that enveloped me.

I tried to reach Dr. Davis and the other men Wilson had suggested. Flags were sent to them, letters asking for some reaction, calls to their offices. Secretaries answered, sometimes answering services; always no response came back, no return call, no letters. It was different with Davis though. He picked up the call from his answering service and returned it, wanting to know what was wanted of him. I told him his name had been suggested by someone at the Urban League and reviewed what my letter had already told him about the flag. I asked if we might talk further about it. He said he'd be in New York in a few days and gave me the name of his hotel. He would meet with me there if it were possible to work it into his schedule.

Days later I called the hotel, got through the switchboard to him and heard his voice say, "Good morning and God bless you."

The conversation took off and flew from that greeting. Davis had my letter and the flag in front of him and was interested in talking more. He asked me to come to his hotel.

When I arrived and asked for Dr. Davis, the bellboy pointed him out to me. Davis was in the lobby waiting for me and having the first advantage of knowing who I was before I met him. That signalled caution on his part but it carried no negative overtones as I found that his interest in the project was genuine and deep. We talked for perhaps half an hour, he listening intently as I ran through highpoints that had happened with the flag right up to the developing plans for the campaign with the Strings.

"You've covered a lot of territory, Mr. Charles. I don't know how much I can help you, but I would like to try. There's never been anything like this before. It's interesting. I'm interested."

Davis' voice was smooth, melodic, taking and holding attention. It was a pleasure to listen to him as he spoke the words I wanted to hear for so long from someone of authority and position. Davis was associated with the *Christian Science Monitor,* a connection that grew out of his being a minister as well as a noted author of black history. He was at ease with words, with people and with situations out of the ordinary and he would prove to be a worthy asset to the group in the coming months. For now, it was refreshing to talk with someone who expressed interest in the flag and a willingness to work in whatever way he could.

He asked about contacts that had been made with organizations and with people of importance in the black community in general. He seemed to feel that my efforts to reach out, so far, had been appropriate even if rejected and he shared with me his sense that it would not be easy to acquire that full recognition of the flag that had eluded me. The campaign that was underway was, in his estimation, a positive step and he encouraged efforts to make it a reality. He wanted to know more about the group and Mabel Morton and wondered whether a meeting could be arranged soon.

The man was a scholar, the kind of achiever black children should read about and have the opportunity to meet. I felt fortunate indeed that fate and a rejection at the Urban League had led me to him. When Davis said he'd stay over an extra day so that he could talk with the group I was pleased.

It went well the next day. Joe greeted Davis with the words, "Mel said you're the most positive person he has spoken to in months and he's delighted that you're interested in what we're trying to do. I just want you to know that we are very pleased that you've taken the time to come here and talk with us."

Davis' response was cautious but open. "I'm not sure what I can do. This project comes suddenly to me but I am interested in discussing it with you."

Again we talked about the flag. Davis was deliberate in his responses, taking time to phrase his questions about our activities so that we revealed to him both the plans and the inner motivation that led us to this point. As he left Davis said, "Mel, I think you have an excellent idea here and if at all possible, if my schedule permits, I will work with you."

He was a busy man, flying between Chicago, Boston and Florida offices and homes, on the move constantly with a schedule that would have challenged the health of a younger man. He gave me his telephone numbers in both Chicago and Boston and told me that I could reach him at one of them during the week. His sharing of ways to reach him was a good sign it seemed to me. Still, my experience had been so often that I would call, talk with someone, and that someone would disappear around the bend before the phone was back in its cradle. It was a frustrating way to live, expecting to be disappointed as each new opportunity presented itself, but it had been a very real experience repeated over and over. It was important that this man come through; his quiet air of competence and self-assurance had been energizing to each of us. We needed that quality of scholarship and intellect be possessed. We needed him.

Several days later he did come through, calling to say, "Tell the men that whenever they are ready I'll come to work with them".

With that call the group reached its full complement of participants, a composite of individuals who would steer the project through the next few months.

Twenty minutes after that message from Davis, while the office still reverberated with the excited talk of Joe and Ted, another call was put through. Bill was on the phone telling me to get ready to go to Cleveland to hear the Strings in performance at a junior high school. Cleveland? He and I had made the trip to Pittsburgh to hear them in rehearsal a few days earlier and had come back with a bit of worry. They had known we were coming and each knew that it was just a rehearsal. We had not expected performance-quality work, but we had found them to be under-rehearsed in the school on the side of a hill in Pittsburgh's black community. The nun in charge, Sister Francis Assisi, was a whirlwind of force and stern discipline as she brought the baton up. The children were excited that "people from New York" were sitting at the back of the auditorium but had gone through the rehearsal valiantly. It was clear that the group had tremendous potential: tone quality was evident, timing good, the repertoire practiced that day showed variety, the nun's command of the children was obvious.

I had felt that we were on the right track, that with the intense rehearsals that would take place between then and the April appearance in New York, the Ozanam Strings would give the performances we wanted and would do them in a very respectable manner. I had felt less concern than had Bill on the flight back from Pittsburgh. He sank into his seat and murmured, "We're in trouble."

"What do you mean?"

"They need more rehearsal than I thought. Time is running out."

"Hey, they're kids, well-trained kids. That nun will pull it off."

"Yeah? You a musician or something?"

"Yes, I am. I know that they have both the potential and the spirit to come through. They'll be okay. Don't forget, Bill, they want to make as good impression on New York as they can. Their name is on the line with this, too."

"Hope you're right, Mel. Right now I'm scared."

He was right; he was scared. This was a classic case of the public relations man's jitters. He was organizing right to the tee and dependent on someone else to come through with the performance he was hyping. All the detail work in the world would have no pay-off if the performers were lousy. He had a legitimate worry. I was just as secure in my own senses that while they had a way to go to be ready for April, they would get there on schedule.

So, why go to Cleveland? Bill insisted. And, my faith in the ability of the nun and the children to be ready was justified. The trip to Cleveland yielded positive results. The audience in that junior high school was small but the music was tremendous, filling the auditorium with the melodic line of the strings. The children themselves presented a compelling appearance massed on the stage wearing their red blazers, black trousers or skirts, crisp white blouses and shirts. From the smallest child, about seven years old, to the tallest young man of seventeen, they exhibited total concentration on their director and their instruments. It was a joy to see this performance.

My Monday call to Bill relayed my enthusiasm about their readiness for the campaign. His sigh of relief could be heard throughout the office.

Joe was brimming with pleasure as I reported on the trip and he agreed with me that we should send a quantity of emblems to Pittsburgh to be sewn on their blazers so that at arrival the connection with the flag would be immediate and obvious. We sent the decals with a listing of the complete itinerary for the week and asked that someone come again to New York to settle final details and arrangements with us. Pitts returned to spend a day in meetings, smoothing into place the details that would lead to a rewarding week for the children. He was anxious to reassure himself that the schedule would not tax the children and that full protection would be afforded for every move that was made. He was more then pleased as the agenda was reviewed and left us that evening with a complete meeting of minds reached.

The Strings were in place and ready for performance: the itinerary had been given full approval. It remained only to work out the little details that any campaign lasting more than an hour required: arrangements with the bus company to assure prompt delivery and pick-ups of the children, assigning children and adult chaperones to rooms in the hotel, securing a photographer to make a visual record of each event, firm-up calls to the United Nations, the Port Authority, Madison Square Garden, the Brooklyn Diocese, the Apollo Theatre. Each day was spent in putting one more detail into place and then checking with Bill, or he with us to report progress on each step. The thin edge of hysteria that can overtake even the most organized and experienced manager of a campaign began to seep into the atmosphere. The manufacturers were pushing their machines, churning out quantities of buttons, decals, emblems to be placed with street vendors for sale in front of the Apollo. Decisions were required as to the most desirable packaging for distribution to these vendors and for setting up a system for them to report in their sales. Display boards and posters had to be made and materials ordered for that purpose. I was personally going to make each of the display boards, backed in velvet and bordered with gold trim. We checked distances and necessary travel time between points in the city so we could be sure that the schedule could work. The details mounted up by the day, requiring more and more energy as April approached.

My hours grew longer each day, extending far beyond the time at which

Joe normally closed the office. I was tired but it was a good tiredness coming from a sense of accomplishment as each day's news was of forward progress.

Toward the end of March, Mabel sat in a meeting listening quietly as we hammered a few more details into place. At the end she took me aside to suggest again that we make a trip to Washington within a day or two. She never said that she thought a break was needed, that a change in the daily grind of preparation would be good for me but, as usual, she filled her role of balancing cog in the wheel of the group. Her suggestion to contact the Urban League had resulted in Dr. Davis' joining the group and so had been productive in that unexpected way. Her suggestion now that we go see the flag on display in Charles Diggs' office and see who we could talk with would give me a break from the pressure as April 3rd neared.

I took her idea seriously this time and peeled off into some hasty calls to Washington, trying to reach the offices of those Congressmen who had responded to my letters, arranging for brief meetings with them during the few hours we would spend there. Mabel took a day off from her work and we flew from LaGuardia to Washington, using the brief flight to speculate on what results we might get from the trip. There had been positive responses from the offices of Augustus Hawkins, Diggs, and Louis Stokes and a couple of others. If we were able to see each of these men our day would be full.

As the plane circled to land I looked at the city below, thinking how few Americans took the time to visit the nerve-center of the country and how many fewer still, had the opportunity to talk with the men who represented them in Congress. Washington was, to most Americans, a never-never land of power, money, and largesse that flowed in the form of income-tax refunds, school lunches, Head Start, grant money, hospitals, roads. While the galleries of Congress were often full, there had never been enough Americans to see the machinery of law-making in motion, to hear the men and women who represented us, to feel first-hand the bustle of power exerted in the constant struggle for balance between the arms of our government. We, as a people, stood in the cradle of those arms, giving ourselves over through our votes to the men and women whose use and manipulations of power led to the tangible results we saw in our communities. It was good to be able to say to myself that I was going to see some of the inner corridors and offices and people whose faces had seemed so distant on television or in the papers. Mabel had been right. This trip was revitalizing even though the plane had not yet landed.

We took a cab to Capitol Hill, finding our way first to Congressman Diggs' office and coming face to face with the first disappointment of the day. Diggs was not there; an important roll-call vote was taking place and he was on the floor of Congress. His secretary recognized our names and gave us some recompense for the disappointment in not seeing Diggs. First, she wanted my autograph! That was a first for me and it was exciting to take the slip of paper and inscribe good wishes to her and sign my name.

Then she asked whether we wanted to see his office and the flag. We jumped at the chance and could hardly wait for her to move the heavy door aside. The offices was furnished quietly, soothing colors on the walls, heavy solid wood furniture gleaming and there on the far wall facing us was the American flag on the left, a Michigan State flag on the right and the Black American Heritage Flag centered on the wall behind his desk! It was on display just as he had said.

That was a powerful moment for me, a time to stand in silence and just let the feeling of pride sweep over me, a pride that surged from the moment the door was opened and the first glimpse into the office revealed the flag in such a prominent place. It didn't matter so much that the Congressman was busy; in fact, it was good to know that business of the nation so occupied him that he was prompt in answering a roll-call and couldn't see me. When Mabel and I turned to thank the secretary for letting us see the office, we were deeply appreciative of that special moment we had just experienced.

We left the office, intent on getting to Augustus Hawkins and bumped into Charles Diggs! He was hurrying to see his secretary for a moment. Obviously having little time, he stopped to let us introduce ourselves. He appeared to recognize our names, thanked me for the flag, and apologized for not being able to spend any time with us. He wound up by saying, "Sorry I have to run, but I want you to know I'm fully behind what you're doing." With those words he turned into his office.

We walked down the hall congratulating each other on having had the chance to see him, but soon found ourselves taking more time between words as we looked at the expanses of corridor before us, woods shining, windows gleaming, brass plates burnished and catching the morning light, wreathing the names of the occupants of the offices with haloes of sparkling importance. We found ourselves wandering the halls, entranced by the solid feel and look of power exemplified in the briskly-moving men and women who served the Congressmen.

Finally we began to seek Augustus Hawkins' office deliberately, only to discover that he, too, was at the roll-call vote. As assistant responded to us, taking a few minutes to talk about the letter and flag I had sent. He didn't seem to know just what the flag was supposed to represent and we plunged in, as usual, to take advantage of an ear that was tuned to us for the moment. We spent about half an hour with him, enjoying the opportunity to discuss the flag in that setting.

From there we sought Louis Stokes' office, by now hoping only half-heartedly that we might find him free to talk. He, too, was in chambers and again we found an assistant who smiled, told us the office had received the package and then began sidling into left field when asked if there were some endorsement or support or leads or encouragement the Congressman could offer. He hemmed and hawed over my request for names of possible contacts and finally said he'd take my name and address. He indicated that he would call New York to recommend people in the Cleveland area who might be amenable to assisting with publicity in that vicinity.

Mabel tried to boost my sagging spirits when we left that office.

"Think positively, Mel. These are busy people. Their days aren't spent waiting for you to come and ask for their support. They have constituencies to represent and not one of them is YOUR Congressman."

"But they're black Congressmen, first of all. And they have some sort of obligation to respond to what a black person asks and I don't care whether he's from Tampa or Toledo. We don't have many to look to and it looks like they have lost touch with us."

"You're impatient, Mel. You want them to turn their day topsy-turvy because you're here."

She was right but my pent up feelings of frustration were on the surface. I had expected so much to come out of this trip and so I vented all of that frustration on Mabel.

"They knew we were coming. We didn't know this vote would come up and I can understand why they aren't personally available. But they could have been ready to give something in the way of support or encouragement. Just a name, a lead, something."

"Why don't you wait and see if something comes up from one of them later. You've condemned them already. Slow down. Wait for just a little while."

"How long? Wait how long? Check the mail every day and then sit on thumbs and wait some more? You're right, I'm impatient. The letters this year weren't the first sent to Congressmen and the responses have been so few and far between that, yes, I'm impatient for someone to bend a little and do something more than shake my hand and let me take a picture. I want endorsement, someone of importance like them to say publicly that the flag has worth and merit and recommend it to black people. It would help if one of these men would stand forward and give it endorsement. Look, Mabel, I'm not asking for anything more than that or some direction to other contacts. I don't want a big speech in Congress and it doesn't need a resolution presented and put in the hopper. Doesn't one of them have the good gut feeling that the flag is important for black people so he'd get out front to say it?"

"Slow down, Mel. You're pushing too hard."

"There's no such thing as pushing too hard on this. If you don't make an effort to move this thing, it will sit on a shelf and mold and that's not what I want."

"That's not what any of us want. The flag will make it. You must give it and yourself time to do what must be done to bring it to the public eye in the way you keep stressing positive, dignified, prideful ways. Today hasn't been a failure. It's been a lesson. You've seen the exercise of responsibility when those men moved to answer a roll-call vote. Isn't responsibility one of the things the flag is supposed to represent?"

I laughed. Again she was right. And I was being unfair in using the day and its circumstances to vent so harshly the feelings that had been building for so long. This had to be let go for now.

"Okay, say no more. I buy it. For now. But I know we won't hear from that assistant or his boss and you know it too."

She smiled. She did know it and we were right. There was never a word from them, except an extraordinary request that came from Diggs later.

There was no point in bursting into the offices of anybody else. These three stops had been planned in advance, letters and telephone calls to make appointments had been acknowledged and fate had handed important business to these men just as we arrived. So, I seized on the positives as much as possible and enjoyed the ride in the open subway cars from building to building, sparkling clean tracks and spit-and-polish seats and rails. It was interesting to see people and to put together a name to whisper to Mabel as we passed the more recognizable of the Congressman we saw.

On the flight back I tried to relax and assess quietly what the day had produced.

Despite the disappointment, it had been worthwhile. A day like this, spent walking through the halls of Congress was a time to absorb the sights and sounds of America's heart in action, sights and sounds that were not usually banked in the memories of most Black Americans. We had not seen many black faces as we walked along through the day. That was a particular sorrow - that so few of us were able to follow our dollars to the Capitol and see what happened to them or watch our votes materialize into the flesh and blood of real people who take seriously the mandates that their constituencies gave them. That there had been no time for discussion of the flag on this day was not their greatest concern.

The trip to Washington had led into a blind alley. That was the bottom line when I talked with Joe and the others the next day.

"Okay. What's next?"

They didn't let up. If this didn't work, the next one would. Call it optimism, positive thinking or maybe just an acceptance of the immediate and a preparation for the coming that was a particular characteristic of people in business. "Split milk sours fast and you get sick if you drink it", their attitudes seemed to say. It was time to move on to the next possibility. You can't stand still.

A day or two later another possibility did appear. Alton Davis had provided a number of new avenues he thought worthy of being pursued. His questions about the history of the flag always focused on Who had been contacted, What had been the outcome? He was visibly dismayed to discover the range of contacts that had taken place in the early days and their lack of fruitfulness. He still had, though, a reservoir of possibilities and shortly after he had joined the project he outlined that list to me. It contained the names of several black historians and he stressed that the major reason for suggesting them lay in his belief that there had never been a banner designed purposefully to represent black people in the history of this country. He felt that if I could secure from established black historians some confirmation of that fact, efforts at promotion of this one would become easier. With that in mind I actively pursued the names on the list, writing, sending the usual package of brochures, clippings, and a small flag. In each mailing went a request that the receiver affirm if at all possible, the uniqueness of the flag. Davis' list also contained the names of prominent ministers, owners of book stores in black communities and the heads of several organizations, including Dr. Charles Wesley, from whom a response had been received not long before the trip to Washington.

Davis thought that omitting a visit to the office of the association for the Study of Negro Life and History while we were there might have been a mistake. He suggested renewing the contact with Dr. Wesley even if it meant another trip to Washington. There were now only days before the Strings were due to arrive in New York and there was still a mountain of things to be done in preparation. But when a telephone call to Dr. Wesley resulted in an invitation to visit him, it was important to all of us that I return to Washington. There was always the feeling that some door would open and if it were possible to get from Dr. Wesley anything that would add to the publicity forthcoming from the campaign, it would be worth the try. The most compelling reason for going though, was that the organization Dr. Wesley served was probably the one most likely to be in a position to affirm the flag's singularity.

I made the trip alone. Mabel was tied up at her work. Davis was not in town. It was a good day to take the train and watch the New York-Washington corridor unfold in a line of small houses and open country as the steady click of the wheels created a sort of mantra that calmed and relaxed me.

The terminal in Washington was busy, people on the move to their appointments on a bright, sunny day. Getting a cab was a problem and it was necessary finally to share one with a young white man who was trying to get to a lobbying session on business for a New Jersey-based company. We had struck up a conversation as we tried to hail cabs separately and agreed that our best bet was to take the first one we could and hope that our destinations would not make either of us late for our appointments. As it happened, the route the cab driver outlined would get me to my address first. I sat through the ride thinking that my companion in the cab would be duly impressed when we reached the association's building. It was quite a letdown when the cab pulled up to a smallish white building located in a residential area and the driver said, "Here it is, buddy!" I peered around the door preparing to tell him he was wrong when I spotted a small plaque and realized I was indeed at my destination.

Wesley was cordial, greeting me in the office that constituted the association's headquarters. It was a place that did not fit any of my preconceptions about what I would find. It was not a library, not a museum. It was a crowded office, books everywhere, hardly any place to hold up the flag much less display it even if permission could be gotten to exhibit it there.

Dr. Wesley's letter to me had made no commitments; he had indicated in our telephone conversation that he was available to meet. Once more then, my usual speech would have to be given, this time with the hope that it would sway him into giving whatever assistance he could. First and foremost was the need to confirm the uniqueness of the flag; secondly I wanted to ask of him, as with everyone else in the history of the flag, any leads to persons or organizations who might be able to assist in the promotion of the flag.

Wesley responded fully to the first question. The flag was unique! The second request ran into the same slow-motion cautious response that characterized my approach to almost everyone who had extensive contacts in the black community or connections that were viable with people of power in the white world. Wesley could offer no assistance with contacts or further leads to individuals. The one thing he did mention that would take substance in the near future was the possibility of placing the flag on display at the Schomburg Museum in New York City. When he asked if I had tried that, my negative answer led him to volunteer a name - Jean Houston - the Director of the Museum. He suggested that I contact her, request exhibit space and use his name as entree. That was helpful of him; it may have been only a gesture but it was more help than many others had given. I thanked him and promised to let him know what results we got when the contact with the Schomburg was made.

Alton Davis was pleased with the results of the meeting with Dr. Wesley and seconded the suggestion to try for exhibit space at the Schomburg. Letters, telephone calls, steady requests for an appointment were put into motion until an opening appeared and Ms. Houston agreed that the flag warranted display in the museum. But all that took place after the Ozanam Strings came through in full form for us in April.

The last few days before the kick-off and the Ozanam Strings' New York debut were lost in a whirlwind of activity.

Bill was in constant contact with me and the group. By March 29, everything seemed to be in place: Honi Coles had confirmed that Nancy Wilson and Cannonball Adderley were amenable to being presented flags publicly at the end of their performances. The children were to perform first, followed by a movie then the guest stars. There was a flurry of telephone calls to Pittsburgh to get the director and Pitts to select some of the older members of the Strings to make the presentations not only to Nancy Wilson and Cannonball Adderley, but to Percy Sutton, Willis Reed, the Ambassador from Liberia, and the other sports figures Bill said would be available at stops along the itinerary.

Bill had shored up details of the schedule including all the performances, the recreational activities, lunches, dinners, hotel rooms and transportation. He kept the group advised of each move as he gulped lunch on the run, made thousands of telephone calls, ran through the routes at the height of rush-hour traffic to double-check travel times, made personal checks on each segment of the agenda from seats in restaurants to determining how many children would be able to get into the Ambassador's office. Bill had pulled it all together. We were as ready as we could be.

It seemed incredible that there were only hours left before the arrival of the bus from Pittsburgh carrying the children of the Strings and their chaperones. Months of planning, conferring, meetings, decisions, questions, and tensions were about to deliver four days of intense activity that would make or break the flag. It was just that simple. If we had ignored some detail that would create negative publicity, if there were some contingency for which we had not foreseen a panacea, if there were any move that would result in injury to person or property, we would be in serious trouble. The welfare of the children was paramount; the opportunity to present the flag in the most dignified and positive light possible was equally important.

It was pointless to worry as April 3rd approached. Everyone was edgy, tired, anxious. It made good sense when Joe suggested that we ought to close shop early on the evening of March 31, the Friday night before the whole thing would start. He thought everybody should go home and take it easy. I still had something to do though; the last of the display boards for the street vendors had to be finished. After Joe said goodnight, I spent a couple of hours in the solitude of the office, arranging and rearranging the buttons and emblems and decals on the boards until the last of my energy was spent. It would be necessary to come back to the office on Saturday morning to meet the vendors and give them their boards and boxes of wares, but that wouldn't take too much time out of the day. I would be able to go home and relax after that last task was done.

I stacked the boards in a corner and turned off the lights and left the building. Davis was at his hotel, Joe and Ted and the others at their homes. Mabel called to say everything would be all right.

There was nothing else to do. Bill had taken care of the details; the big things would take care of themselves.

Chapter 13

Joy chattered in the seat beside me as we drove into New York on the afternoon of April 3rd. She had been barely able to contain herself all day in anticipation of going into the city with me to meet the bus bringing the Ozanam Strings. She knew these were children important to me but that she was the one who would be standing with me when they arrived.

We talked on the ride over, taking the chance to catch up on some school events she had been participating in and enjoying. It was a pleasant drive, and her conversation was a relief. It was good to listen to talk of school plays and spelling bees for these last few minutes before it would all begin. Route 1 faded away before I knew it and we were on the downslope of the ramp leading through the mouth of the Holland Tunnel.

I glanced toward Joy and past her, my attention caught by a group of black men standing near a trash-can fire at the first traffic light island. Their hands were extended over the fire as they waited for a trucker to stop and offer them a few dollars to ride into the city and help unload cargo. Three men were there, thin coats pulled tightly around them as the cold April winds blew. Their eyes roved the lines of traffic, searching for the eighteen-wheelers and the chance to make a sawbuck. They jumped up and down a little, demonstrating their agility. One driver nodded and all three started towards his rig. He lifted his hand from the wheel and pointed to the oldest of the men and that one sprinted through the lines of cars and climbed into the cab of the truck. It was over in less than fifteen seconds. One man had a job for a few hours and two more had to wait their turn.

It was a slave block. The whole scene was a throw-back that was ridiculous. Grown, black men prancing to show their strength to earn meager pay. The man who got the nod thought he was lucky. He'd been chosen because he was the oldest one there and would accept the least pay from the driver.

"What are you looking at, Daddy?"

"Nothing, Joy. Nothing and everything."

"Oh, Daddy, how can something be nothing and everything at the same time?"

My answer was lost in the blast of a car horn behind us; some driver was impatient with my failure to move the three feet that had opened in front of my car. Only a couple more cars stood between us and the last cross street and it would be free and clear to the toll booth. The light changed and we were caught once again. I glanced out the window to the left at a van turning into the cross street. A large black arm was raised, shackled to another, handcuff banging on the window of the van to get my attention. I saw the clenched fists and read the words being mouthed by the man. "Right on, brother." The arms fell and one hand pointed to the decal on the window of my car, a decal that read "Black Is Beautiful - Black American Heritage Flag." It was then that the van completed its turn and sped off, bold letters on its back telling everyone that it was a New Jersey Correctional Division vehicle.

Black men standing on a corner waiting to hustle mean pay for hard labor. Black men giving a black power salute as they were carted off to jail. It was nothing and everything at once. The futility of life for so many black people was beginning to sour the day before it could get started.

"Daddy, you didn't answer my question. How..."

"Joy, do you know why we're going into New York?"

"Yes, Daddy. Today is when the Ozanam Strings come to play for you and the flag."

"Well, that's the everything. The nothing is that they shouldn't have to come to New York to play for the flag. The flag should have been around for a long time for them and for you and for everybody who is black. The nothing is that we have been treated as though we didn't even exist. That's the real nothing."

"I don't understand the last part of what you said, Daddy."

"Baby, I hope you will one day. I know you will. But for now, just enjoy the ride and meeting the children. You're going to like them."

"I know it. I'm glad they're coming."

I was too. It was the day of days. All the months of preparation were focused on today and the harvest that would come home from the labors of a lot of people.

The cars moved as the light turned. The toll booth and tunnel were ours. The day had begun.

The bus was scheduled to arrive at 6:00 p.m. Everybody was waiting in the lobby of the hotel, a cast assembled in the wings listening to their surging heartbeats and counting the seconds until the curtain went up. Joe tried every chair in the lobby, finally finding one that gave him comfort and ease and his quiet smile radiated out to each of us. Vic and Ted stood near the door. Morty Kliemann, one of the manufacturers peripheral to BLAM but active in some of the meetings, wanted to join us in the planning of the week's activities and we welcomed his involvement. Joy attached herself to Mabel, chattering away as she made a new friend. Bill moved from one to the other of us, repeating over and over to himself the agenda for the evening.

"They're Here!"

I don't know who said the words but they galvanized each of us. Everybody moved to the door and into the sidewalk as the bus rolled to a stop and the faces of the children filled the windows, smiling and waving.

Bob Pitts was first off the bus, hand extended, a big smile on his face. Sister Francis Assisi was next, demure, exuding confidence. She stood at the door to help the smallest of the children off the bus and suddenly the sidewalk was filled with a sea of red blazers and awestruck children, their heads craning backwards to take their first good look at the skyscrapers of the city. Their excitement at stepping foot onto the pavement of New York was palpable. They nudged each other, whispering comments at the sights they were seeing even in those first few minutes. It took some time to get them into the hotel and to their rooms with their chaperones. It was clear that Pitts and the other chaperones were as anxious for the children to exhibit their best behavior as we were for them to be successful performers and exemplary guests. It took only a word from him and there was silence and brisk movement to whatever spot the moment called for. This good sign pleased me. The disciplined behavior seen in Pittsburgh and Cleveland was even more in evidence here in New York. The nun and the chaperones had done a masterful job of preparing the children for this appearance. The schedule for that Monday night was tight. As soon as they were checked in, it was time for dinner and the bus to Brooklyn and the performance at the church.

I didn't go to Brooklyn with them. A tiredness overcame me, tiredness born of constant movement over the last several days as we had gone from place to place checking out the itinerary and arrangements. It seemed better to take that evening and go home and get some rest. It was obvious that there would be little solitude or stillness over the next four days. Tearing Joy away from newly-made friends was difficult. She had melted into the group of younger children and found the instant camaraderie that sometimes eludes adults. She was promised that she would come back the next day to go on the Circle Line excursion with the children and reluctantly she left with me, falling asleep in the car almost as soon as we got in it.

Early the next morning we were back in New York. She was anxious to see her new friends; I, eager to hear how the performance had gone at the church. Bill was at the hotel waiting to tell me that the audience had been impressed and the Strings "fantastic". He was pleased that this first performance had gone so well, that the promise had been fulfilled. "Everything is going just right, Mel," he said.

It did, too, that day. The sun was shining in a clear sky as the bus arrived on schedule and the children talked excitedly as we made our way to the pier to board the Circle Line ship that would provide the first recreational activity for the Strings. They filled the ship, moving from rail to seat to hotdog stand and back to the rails. The changing views of New York engaged both children and adults. The Strings fell silent as we passed near the Statue of Liberty and gasped in amazement as they saw the huge ships docked at piers and the little tug-boats that defied belief as they moved other ships to channels for safe passage out into the ocean.

There was so much to see including the Strings themselves. Other passengers were fascinated by the large group of children dressed in their red blazers with the emblem of the flag carefully sewn in place. Passengers asked questions - "Who are they? Where are they from?" Often the children responded proudly, pleased to announce that they would be performing over the next few days. Their pride in themselves was obvious but not overbearing. I stood at the rail and watched them and felt good about our bringing them to New York.

They were to play at the Apollo that afternoon and the schedule called for them to take a short break after the excursion, just enough to tamp down the excitement of the boat ride and to build a new tension, the kind of tension that is necessary for a good performance.

The schedule worked. At 4:00 pm. the bus unloaded the group at the

Apollo Theatre. The children stood quietly on the sidewalk waiting for directions to enter. They were an impressive sight, violin cases held tightly, complete uniforms bright and eye-catching, order and discipline marking them as performers ready for the coming hours. They watched with interest as the street vendors arrived, opened their boxes and folding tables and set themselves up on the sidewalk outside the theatre. The kids gave a cheer as they realized that the vendors' wares were all related to the flag. The men grinned at the children and mockingly offered decals and buttons for sale to them. Everyone was high-spirited.

It took an hour to get into the theatre and set up for the performance. Stands had to be brought off the bus, instruments taken from their cases and tuned, the piano positioned to meet the firm directions of the Sister, children instructed on their entry points to the stage. The theatre was dark and empty when we entered; it was only partially filled at 5:00 p.m. when the baton came down and the Strings began to play.

People trickled in throughout the first hour of performance. The appearance of the Strings was not what had brought them to the theatre; it was the promise of hearing the voice of Nancy Wilson and the music of Cannonball Adderley that turned out the eventually packed house. We had known that there would be a crowd to hear them and had counted ourselves fortunate that they had been billed for that evening. A full house was what we wanted to witness the presentations of the flags and to see the talents of black youngsters doing something quite different from anything that had ever been on the stage of the Apollo.

The Strings had been scheduled to play for an hour to be followed by the movie and then the guest stars. As it happened, by the time the performance should have ended, the theatre was packed with people who had heard only one or two pieces and whose applause told everyone they wanted to hear more. That applause flooded backstage into the wings where I stood watching the nun and the kids reach into a great reservoir of playing strength and pour it out in what was to have been their finale. The soloists were introduced and took their bows and still the audience applauded for more. Honi Coles moved beside me and stood watching and listening for a few minutes and made the decision to let the Strings keep playing. The nod went to the nun and she turned back to the children, put her finger to her lips, then told them quietly that they would continue to play. The children were pleased; they were playing well and enjoying it. The applause had stimulated their desire to stay on stage and they were as eager as they had been when they began to play.

The movie was never shown that night. The Strings played until 7:30, moving first one then another child to center front as soloist, the pianist among them stretching his hands to do incredible things with the instrument, playing in a way that would do justice to a mature, seasoned performer rather than the 16-year old, rangy kid who sat there. The audience responded openly, yelling shouts of appreciation, applauding gustily and continually as the bows moved across the strings of the violins. It was an exceptional performance, almost eerie in a way to see how well the audience responded to the children, the instruments so unique to that stage and the music they performed. When the house lights finally came up at the end, Joe and Ted and the others could be seen sitting up front, beaming with pleasure.

It took a few minutes to move the children off stage and into seats scattered throughout the audience. In those few minutes everything belonging to the Strings was moved to the bus and the stage prepared for the evening's star performers. The stage crew was good; the professional performers outstanding. The children were excited as they watched. Some hopped out of their seats to stand near the walls to get a good view, relishing the chance to watch the ways a seasoned trouper gets and holds the attention of an audience.

The bill opened with a ventriloquist - a young, black man who handed us a double treat. He was not only talented; he gave us an unexpected boost with his act. He had entered holding the dummy with its back to the audience until he was seated and ready to start. Then suddenly he turned it around and there on its chest was a huge Black American Heritage Flag button. The "dialogue" was moving as they "talked" about the beauty of being black and young and talented. It was quite an experience to hear and see the act.

Nancy Wilson and Cannonball Adderley took the house down -- she with the powerful voice contradicting the diminutive figure in the middle of the spotlighted stage, and he with the clean pure sound driven out note by note like bullets from a machine gun. In their separate acts they demonstrated the range and versatility of the talents possessed by black people.

Immediately after Adderley finished it was time to make the presentations of the flags. Two of the older members of the Strings had been selected to represent the group and the boys were polished and ready to say the words that summed up their feelings about the performances they had seen and how that strengthened their belief in the flag's representing all that was positive and good about black people. Adderley took his with a musician's compliments to other musicians, a flattering gesture to the young boys making the presentation. Honi Coles was called out of the wings, a surprise to him. When he was presented a flag he spoke eloquently, commending the youngsters for their performance and for their shining example of what black children could do given the opportunity.

Nancy Wilson had been fighting laryngitis and was unable to return to the stage to receive her flag. Coles indicated that she would be available backstage if we wanted to go there to see her. When the word spread among the children, several slipped along behind me and the two who were to make the presentation, climbing over the ropes and around the props stacked against the walls. The dim light barely outlined the path we followed to get to the steps but somehow the children and I managed to make it up to where she was waiting. The photographer we had hired to record every move made by the Strings was there to take pictures of this presentation. He was as surprised as I to find that her "dressing room" was a curtained-off corner of the upper room, affording her little privacy. But she was gracious within that limited space, posing for pictures and talking with the children who crowded around her.

As we prepared to leave we caught a glimpse of Cannonball Adderley over in his dressing area. He was caught up in a friendly but heated discussion with someone who wanted to take his flag. We saw him fold it and tuck it under his jacket and heard him say that it was his and when he left the theatre that night it was going with HIM and nobody else!

The evening was a success! The children had played exceptionally well, the audience had been responsive to them and to the public presentations of the flag, the guest stars had been more than gracious in their acceptances. Joe, Ted, Vic, Morty, Bill, Mabel and I had gathered on the sidewalk to congratulate ourselves as the bus left with the Strings headed for the hotel. We were all pleased that things had gone so well and spoke excitedly of the events of the next day, sure that the rest of the schedule would be as rewarding as this had been.

Percy Sutton's office was first on the agenda for Wednesday. The children were up bright and early, eager to be on their way to the activities that were intended for their pleasure, their chaperones delighted to see that what we had promised we were delivering -- an agenda that was planned as much for the enjoyment of the children as it was for promotion of the flag.

The office of the Manhattan Borough President was impressive. A huge conference table dominated the center of the room, but it was the view of the city from the window that beckoned the children. They stood behind Sutton's desk, absorbing the sights of the East River, the Manhattan and Brooklyn Bridges, and the skyline that presented itself. They were buzzing quietly about the view when Sutton entered the office with his son, a young man in his early twenties. Introductions were made and Sutton launched into a little talk meant for the children's ears, telling them what a borough president was.

He was smooth, his voice pouring out in the unmistakable tones that marked his speech pattern, and he seemed genuinely pleased to have the children as his guests. He talked about talent and the use of it, encouraging them to keep playing, growing, performing, exhibiting the best that they had. His remarks led appropriately to the presentation of a flag, made by one of the children. Then without any announcement, the children of the Strings joined hands in a big circle and began to sing "Reach Out and Touch Somebody's Hand". We had not known that this was their private sign-off when completing a rehearsal and that it had become for them a symbol of their unity and oneness in performance and in spirit. It was a very moving moment when the song ended. Sutton appeared deeply touched by the melody and the words and the innocence of the children. He said good-bye almost reluctantly. Perhaps it was a welcome change for him, having guests in his office who came not to ask favors but to bring him something, a flag and a moment of song. He promised that his office would keep in touch with me and thanked the children for sharing some of their time with him.

They left the office brimming with excited words about the man they had just met, his office and the vistas stretching out from the window. The adults from Pittsburgh had done a good job of preparing them for New York. As the bus neared the United Nations Building it was obvious that the kids recognized it, knew what it represented and appreciated the chance to see in person what had been only a picture until then. We posed for our photographer in front of the bank of flags in the plaza and then formed into lines for the tour.

The building enchanted the children; their questions flowed freely and their response to the guide's directions was flawless. The last stop was at the office of the Liberian Ambassador. He was ready for them, his assistants moving quietly around as the children were shepherded through his offices. They were quiet as they looked at the pictures and artifacts that came from Liberia. Their eyes were big as they got their first glimpse of a real African.

We left the evening free for the children and their chaperones to walk in Times Square. They reacted as any tourist would, excited, completely entranced by the magnetic ambience of the moving signs, the traffic, and the bright lights. We were told that the kids dropped into bed that night, tired, falling asleep instantly and probably with visions of the tinseled wonderland that was the core of New York.

The next day's highlight was the trip to Madison Square Garden where they were to have lunch and meet Willis Reed, captain of the New York Knickerbockers. As we left the hotel, Bill edged in close to me and said, "Mel, I think we're in trouble."

"What do you mean? What's wrong?"

"I don't know whether Reed can make it. It's a big series for the Knicks and for him to have to leave the playoffs at the half, get down to the restaurant and get back in time for the game may be impossible."

"He's got to come through. The kids are going to be disappointed if he doesn't show."

"Yeah, I know. But you know how it is -- the best laid plans can go wrong."

I looked at him and thought that there was more wrong than the possibility that Willis Reed might not be able to get to the restaurant. While I told him, "Well, let's hope for the best," I was wondering where the media coverage was. Bill had assured us that he had taken care of it; the agenda for the appearances of the Strings had been sent to United Press, Associated Press, the television stations' news centers and the newspapers. So far the only photographer who had shown had been the one we had hired. Not one reporter or photographer or camera crew had appeared on the scene and the schedule of appearances was half-over. Joe and the others had opened a newspaper in the office just that morning before we left for the hotel to pick up the Strings. We scanned the paper quickly, then more thoroughly, looking for some mention of the performance at the Apollo, the stop at Sutton's office, something, any attention to the children and by connection to the flag. There was nothing in print.

There was something wrong, all right, and it wasn't that Reed was playing an important game and might not be able to keep the appointment. But the kids were loading into the bus and it was essential to keep to the agenda, enjoy lunch and hope that both Reed and media coverage would materialize on schedule.

As we sat in the restaurant we could hear roars from the Garden. We were finishing dessert as a murmur of sound arose from the children. Willis Reed had come to meet them. The kids were on top of the world at the sight of a genuine black hero. They wanted autographs, looking raptly at the tall, impressive young man who epitomized black basketball players. He got their full attention as he spoke briefly, welcoming them to the Garden, wishing them well in their performances, accepting a flag with pleasure. There was no disappointment among the children and the day wasn't over yet.

After lunch they walked the block to the Empire State Building, eager to see the city from that vantage point, then they took the rest of the afternoon to wander off in small groups with their chaperones to sight-see, window shop and continue to see the sights and sounds of New York. No performances were scheduled for that day; it was planned for their pleasure only.

While the Strings were off sight-seeing, I spent the afternoon with Bob Pitts, talking through the coming television appearance on the Joe Franklin show that night. Bill had followed through on our earlier conversation with Franklin and pinned down a guest slot for Pitts, Dr. Davis and myself. It seemed good promotion to take a three-pronged approach to that appearance: Pitts would talk about the organization and purpose of the Ozanam Strings, Davis would talk about the flag in the context of black history and I would describe the flag itself to the audience.

We were to meet Bill and his wife for dinner prior to the show and go from there to the studio where we were to be met by Dr. Davis, Joe and Mabel. Bob and I arrived at the restaurant in Times Square early. Bill and his wife had not yet arrived so we put off the waitress, thinking to wait for them. Finally we saw Bill headed toward us weaving through the tables. It was not until he was right in front of us that we could see that his weaving walk was the result of too much to drink. His wife hurried up behind him, putting a steadying hand on his waist and eased him into a seat. I was appalled. Bill was drunk!

His first words, "Let's have a drink!" demolished my appetite. There was no way to force anything down my throat; the gorge of anger filling it would not give way. He insisted that we order white wine at least. It sat untouched while Pitts and I tried individually to figure out how we could override this development. There was nothing we could do with Bill; there wasn't enough time to take him somewhere and sober him up. His wife appeared embarrassed and ineffectual to deal with the problem. There was no help for the situation; we had to go through with the show and for now could only hope that he would be able to stand up long enough for us to make it there and out.

We left the restaurant, I wanting to put as much space as possible between myself and the wobbly Bill. When we reached the entrance to the building and found the elevator, it was painfully comical to watch him prop himself against a wall and close his eyes for the short ride. When we got out at the studio it was a relief; Bill could be steered to a seat and we could turn our attention to the directions we would be given for the show.

Davis was there with Mabel and Joe. We joined them just as Joe Franklin came over and asked how things were going. Pitts spoke for all of us telling Franklin that things had been letter-perfect. As they talked I caught a glimpse of Bill, hunched over, head focused near his knees. I thought he was getting ready to go over on his face when suddenly he got up and came toward me, waving a small white index card.

"Here, Mel. This is for you."

"Yeah? What is it?"

"It's a cue card for you. I want you to pin it to the back of the flag and when you hold it up it will have everything on it you need to say."

"I don't need that, Bill. Why don't you just go back and sit down? Everything is going to be all right. Go and sit."

He was too drunk to see my anger and there was no point in making a scene with him. I beckoned to his wife. She came over and retrieved him and they returned to the seats while Pitts, Davis and I waited for our time slot. Once I located that holding area I went back to where Bill and his wife were sitting to get the flag I'd left beside them. Again, I told Bill that everything would go well.

"Relax and enjoy, Bill.

Camera and stage crews moved efficiently, placing cables, lights, chairs, and the small audience in readiness for the show. Someone whispered to me that a woman well-known to television audiences was sitting front center. She was easy to pick out, white hair peeping under a ridiculous hat, rotund figure packed into a dowdy dress. She was greeted as though she were a celebrity by crew and audience alike. She was often referred to by name on some talk shows and she relished their recognition of her. Some people are professional funeral-goers; she had a monopoly on camera-range seats at television programs. After the show, I was told, she gathered an audience around herself to say that she "had never known niggers had accomplished anything in life" and she was very surprised by what she had heard on the show.

Dr. Davis spoke first. He was impeccable as he described the long train of black history in this country in succinct phrases, emphasizing the contributions black people had made to the growth and wealth of the nation. He moved smoothly into describing the first meeting he and I had had, a meeting where he had come to realize that a piece of cloth could be transformed into a symbol of pride and heritage. He felt, he said, there was a story worth hearing about the creation of the flag and he was pleased that we had the opportunity to tell it. Franklin picked up the questioning, asking me to describe the flag.

I held it up and there was the index card, pinned on it while my back was turned! It fluttered as the flag unfolded, stirring my anger again. Part of my mind was focused on that piece of paper and Bill's audacity at pinning it there. My words were etched on my brain, lodged in my gut; I didn't need that paper. But it was there and I would just have to deal with him later.

The description went fairly well. This time, at least, there were no monosyllabic answers to questions. The words flowed as smoothly as possible given the residue of anger that still gripped me.

Pitts described with feeling how the Ozanam Strings came to exist, their pleasure at being invited to New York to help promote the flag as well as the opportunity to perform in the citadel of musicians.

Franklin seemed pleased with the interviews and invited us, while still on the air, to come back and do another show with him. He faced the audience and said that he thought we had just skimmed the surface of black history and pride and that it was worth talking about more in the future. On those words, the program faded into a commercial and we moved off stage. We thanked Franklin for giving us time and told him we would be available to come back anytime to do another show on television or radio.

We moved into the audience just as the young man with the guitar began to perform. We hadn't known that his particular specialty was to take a few words and construct lyrics on an impromptu basis. As we walked toward the back of the studio we realized that the song he was singing was about the flag. We stopped to listen, applauding both his musicianship and his commentary on the flag. It was a good end to the show.

We had been through three full days of activity, spent thousands of dollars, pushed ourselves to the limits of endurance, smiling as each step on the agenda was completed with precision, tossing sleeplessly at night hoping that the next day would go as planned. There was not one of us who did not harbor still some fear that something would go wrong and swallow us in negative publicity yet each was putting on the best face possible, hiding those fears as best we could, digging deep for the energy to make the next stop on the schedule.

The next morning I sped to New York, planning to be at Port Authority when the bus arrived with the children. My timing was good. The van delivered the stands and we had just finished setting up on the mezzanine when word came that the bus had arrived out front. The children moved quietly through the concourse, climbed the steps quickly, moved into place and began to get their instruments ready. Bill had arranged for a couple of football players from the Giants to be there to receive flags and they made their appearance right on time.

The performance was to began a noon. At 11:45 Ted Shaw climbed the steps to the mezzanine. I asked him where Bill was; he hadn't appeared through any of the setting-up process nor was he with the Strings when they arrived. Ted was apologetic, hesitating over the words he didn't want to say.

"Bill is blasted, drunk right out of his head, Mel. The pressure has been too great on him."

I stared at Ted. What did he mean? Was Bill too drunk to take charge of this last appearance of the Strings?

Ted went on without waiting for me to respond to him. "Pressure, Mel, pressure. Bill knows we have sunk a lot of money into this and we're waiting for it to pay off in ink, center section of some paper, and he hasn't been able to produce it. Nothing has worked for publicity. He's buckling under that pressure."

I turned from Ted, too upset to say anything, knowing that it was too late anyway. And there, leaning against a column below us was Bill, his face red, his breathing labored. He was too drunk to stand alone. How he got there was beyond my understanding.

He was of no use at that moment. The important thing was to get the performance underway, the presentations and the program completed.

The Strings played beautifully. The music floated from the mezzanine filling the long concourse with sounds that drew a large and appreciative audience. Applause rang out as each number was finished, the children accepted with deep bows to the audience. Commuters were used to hearing performers play from that mezzanine and perhaps this audience was no larger than usual, but it seemed to me that we had gathered a tremendous crowd of people who stopped their day for a few minutes to enjoy the music that the children made.

It was a shame there was no one from the media to witness the performance. It almost didn't matter that the appearance was promotion for a flag. What did matter was that black children could stand playing an instrument that is classical in its history and hold an audience captive with their performance. They were good and deserved some media coverage just for themselves.

That coverage never materialized. A schedule that had been designed to grab maximum coverage with morning, afternoon and evening performances scattered around the city, had netted exactly one brief mention in the *Daily News* and that was an advance notice of their appearance at the Port Authority Terminal. There was nothing else; not one word, not one picture, not one reporter or camera on the scene at any point.

I left the group as the last of the children boarded the bus to return to their hotel. Everyone had been told that I would see them the following morning before they pulled out of the city. I went home, depressed, upset, angry. The week had gone well, the children had given their best in each performance, each appointment had gone on schedule. All of the people on whom we depended, the stars at the Apollo, basketball players, a Borough President, an ambassador -- they had all come through just as we had planned. And Bill had failed to produce publicity and coverage.

It was painful to think about it. It was impossible to work through my disappointment that night. Some small part of my being refused to deal with it, that part where all my hopes were in hiding, fearful to face the reality of what had happened. It was necessary to wait until there had been a few days interlude before I could put everything into a better perspective.

That next morning I was at the hotel early. It was important to see the Strings off, to thank them for the magnificence of their performances and for the excellent example they had set as they moved around the city. While the children boarded the bus, Pitts took Joe and me aside to thank us. He and the other adults were more than pleased that everything had gone well. He had heard from Pittsburgh; radio and television there had kept up a steady stream of reports on the activities of the Ozanam Strings.

I shook hands with the nun. She was visibly tired but still in charge, moving the children with a snap of the fingers and a firm word. She, too, was pleased and grateful for the experiences that had been provided for the children. We wished each other well and waved as the bus pulled off. The children called out "good-bye" until the bus turned the corner.

Joe and I stood there for a few minutes looking in the direction they had gone, neither of us fully appreciating yet that the week was over, the big promotion campaign ended. We left each other without speaking, not able to talk, wanting only to be alone for a while.

Chapter 14

I spent much of the weekend sitting in the rec room at home, poring over clippings of news articles dating back to the first one in 1967. It was important to find some way to review all the events that had taken place since that Sunday at Gleason's house. Here it was six years later and I was sitting at the table in my basement trying to figure out where that idea had gone in all that time, what had been accomplished, what it was possible to do now. I ran across the letter that a young boy had written soon after the first news article appeared. He wrote that he was proud to know that black men had designed a flag for black people. That boy had grown up and become the youngest member of the Newark Board of Education. I thought about all the old men and women who had encouraged us through those days of trying to bring consciousness of the flag to the surface, days and nights of meeting all requests to talk about the flag. We had gotten encouragement from many fronts. That had offset the back-biting that had come too. Now I was looking at a massive effort, light-years away from the hit or miss efforts of the early years, a campaign that had required huge amounts of money yet still hadn't produced the end result of publicizing the flag enough to reach the millions of black people who would make it have real meaning.

It was hard to sit there and sort out my feelings about the last few days. So much had been accomplished and yet so little. It was true that the Oza-nam Strings had produced what they were expected to produce and that everything on the agenda had taken place as planned and without any problems. As the weekend faded it dawned on me that Bill had really tried. He had developed a plan that should have worked in every dimension. It should have; it just didn't! But why? Had Bill's connections been faulty, had he been the weak link? Or had this whole thing once again been an exercise in the futility of trying to bring something representing black people to the fore and finding that the media was not interested. It was positive without blood or gore, without firebombings or murder, marches or screaming. Did it lack newsworthiness? Was it not worth media time? What had been the problem with getting media exposure? Was it Bill? His connections? The concept of the flag? What?

And what was to happen now? Could there be another attempt like this one or should its failure be taken as a clear signal that not even this kind of effort could produce the results wanted? Were the men going to wash their hands of the whole project? Was this the end of the flag? How many more times could I gather energy to pour into some plan and see it go down the drain?

My mind zig-zagged through the maze of these questions trying to find answers. Soft music that filtered through to my consciousness. I watched the news in an effort to find something of importance that had bumped the campaign from mention in the papers or on TV news reports. There was nothing.

Monday morning at the office everybody tip-toed around everybody else. There was no re-hash, no gathering to dissect the week's events. It was almost as though everyone had sunk into his own personal world and was going through the mechanics of a day at work without any real sense of being there. It was strange not to hear the phone ring with Bill on the other end jumping excitedly into his rush of talk about some plan or contact he had made. My telephone didn't ring at all that morning. Joe kept to his office taking care of business that had been let slide during the previous week.

I looked through a stack of mail half-heartedly. Suddenly there was an envelope in front of me with a House of Representatives return address. It was a letter from Congressman Diggs, a short note asking for a flag for his cleaning lady. She had gotten up the courage to ask him to get one for her and he was carrying through on her request.

Funny how something like that can turn a day around for you. It was the jump-start needed to make the self-pity go away. Here was something to do; get a small flag packaged, addressed, and make the dash to the post-office to mail it personally. It felt good to be making a connection in even this indirect way with someone who had an obvious appreciation for the flag.

When I returned from the post office, I approached Joe and opened a conversation he didn't seem to want to take place.

"We need to meet, Joe. We need to sit down with Bill and talk through what has happened."

"We know what happened!" he replied. "We don't need to meet right now."

"Yes we do. We need to say now what's going to be in the future. I need to know what the group is going to do."

"Okay. We'll make it in a few days. You're right. We do need to talk. I'm just not ready for it right now."

We gathered about a week later. Everyone was there -- Joe, Ted, Vic, Davis, Mabel. Bill had been told to meet with us later that afternoon. We needed to meet first without him.

It was a rough discussion, sharp edges on words as each one reviewed his perceptions of the campaign. There was immediate agreement that the agenda had been fulfilled, that the promise of outstanding performance by the Ozanam Strings had been kept, that everyone on whom the project depended had come through. Except Bill's delivery of publicity. The crux of the campaign was adequate coverage and publicity. We had gotten neither. Bill had not produced. But was that his fault? Here we divided. Some thought he had made the effort and that was what counted. Some saw that as rationalization for the failure to produce publicity. Some blamed Bill personally; others felt that nobody could have moved the media if it wasn't interested.

The bottom line was reached finally. Bill had not produced. Bill had fallen apart in the crunch. Bill had to go! We couldn't get past that point to discuss what would be the group's next efforts to promote the flag. Easing him out of the inn was uppermost in the minds of the members of the group.

It is never easy to cut someone loose and nobody wanted to be the one to tell Bill he was finished, especially since it seemed that it had to be done publicly with the entire group present. Joe was the least prepared to drop the axe; he had found Bill in the first place. Ted, Vic and Morty were clearly too angry to be the ones to tell him. Neither Davis nor Mabel had been involved with the group when Bill was hired; they were not the ones to let him go. I was back in the middle of the circle, faced with the nasty business of making the open statement that we could no longer use his services. It was not a pleasant task that had been laid at my feet.

Davis left the meeting; he was due in Chicago in a matter of hours. It seemed to pain him that he could not stay to help ease me through what was coming. The rest stayed, drifting out to lunch, coming back murmuring quietly about the good things that had happened only days before, wishing aloud over and over that Bill had come through for us.

He arrived right on time, cleanly shaven, face smooth and looking rested.

He smiled jovially as he shook hands and sat down, giving no indication that he expected to be cut loose from the group. He was asked whether he had anything to tell us, anything he wanted to say.

To our great surprise, he jumped to his feet and began to pace the floor as he launched into the most emotional statement we had ever heard, a statement full of commentary on the plight of black people, the need to have a symbol of unity and pride and the rightness of the flag to be that symbol, the urgency to develop a means to bring the flag to the consciousness of both black and white America.

He sounded like he was born-again, the fervor of his words stunning us. It was a beautiful speech. He mesmerized us as he talked about what had to be done, what could be done, the lessons learned from the week's experiences, the need to reach hearts and minds, the time that would have to be given in the future, his willingness to give his all to make the flag a success. He was an orator on a stump by the time he finished. It was difficult not to applaud his performance. He had been somewhere and done some thinking. He was talking the way he should have talked all the weeks he had chattered about taking care of details and letting big things take care of themselves. He almost carried it off. Almost, that is, until he laid out a request for $10,000 to start a second campaign effort.

I could see the dollar signs run past the businessmen in the room, dollar signs that mounted up to the big money that had been paid to Bill every two weeks and the lack of a jackpot at the end of the campaign he had formulated. I looked at each one and saw that they were determined to be rid of Bill and that they were waiting for me to say it.

"Bill, you tried. We know that and we want you to know we recognize all the energy and effort you put into it. We just can't wait any longer.

We can't take another project, another campaign, and see it go down the drain like this one did. No publicity, no coverage, no grand promotion. It got the best of you. The man I saw Thursday at the restaurant and Friday at Port Authority wasn't the Bill I knew. The Bill I knew was straight, keeping on track. You got off somehow and we can't chance it again. We appreciate what you have done but we're severing the connection.

My words fell into silence in the room. Bill was sitting forward on the edge of his chair, eyes never straying from my face. He looked around, reading the faces of the others in the room, knowing that they were in accord with what had been said and that indeed this was the end of the relationship.

He got up awkwardly, buttoned his jacket. Everybody else rose too, shook his hand, and they left. I walked with him to the elevator, wished him luck, thanked him again and watched the doors close on him. I never saw Bill again.

Back at my desk, I called Dr. Davis. He had waited in his Chicago office to know what the outcome of the meeting had been. He asked what would happen next.

"I still want a public relations man, one who can reach the black community, somebody who can move the flag into the black mainstream and do it effectively."

"Have you talked to Billy Rowe?"

"I tried to reach him a couple of months ago after you mentioned his name the first time. I couldn't make a connection with him."

"I'll give you his number. Try him again. Tell him Davis told you to call. If he will meet, let me know and I'll be in New York."

It was worth another try. No one had recovered from the trauma of the campaign, but not one person had given a sign of letting go the commitment to make the flag viable.

I called Rowe and this time got through to him. He showed immediate interest when Dr. Davis' name was mentioned and said he would certainly come to a meeting with us. I sent him a lapel pin with the letter confirming the appointment for the following week.

He was prompt in arriving at Davis' hotel and talked with us earnestly about what he might be able to do to help promote the flag. He had worn the lapel pin to an NAACP conference in Boston a day or two before and he had been impressed by the questions and comments it had aroused in people as he moved around the conference. We asked how he thought he could help. He offered to mention the flag in an upcoming article in the *Afro-American* and then see what followed from that mention.

In due time the article appeared, a few lines buried in his syndicated column but there just the same. When that edition appeared, Rowe called to ask whether we had seen it and what the reaction of the group had been. We hadn't gotten that far - I had to tell him. We needed time to explore what, if anything, they were willing to do at this point, especially the hiring of another public relations man. "Once burned, twice shy" - the words kept running through my head as I asked Joe to call everybody together to hear what Rowe might have to say. He agreed however that this was worth exploring and a meeting was scheduled for the following week.

Rowe arrived, making an impressive entrance. The group was quiet, listening intently as he talked about the span of his contacts and some possibilities that might emerge from his many connections. No commitments were made in that meeting; the need to talk privately among ourselves prevented even a handshake on a possible deal to hire him.

After he left we talked about the probable costs of hiring him and the possible returns from that step. It was clear that the experience with Bill had left a bitter taste and distrust of public relations people in general. Nobody had anything negative to say about Rowe, but nobody wanted to go out on a limb and say "yes, hire him". Not now. The scars were still fresh.

Later that evening I called Rowe. He sensed the distance of the men though he didn't know whether it was mistrust of him or the aftermath of the campaign. He did feel that he had something to offer but his sense that the group was fearful of making a contractual agreement with him gave him little to go on. The fearfulness was real; the businessmen were simply not ready to hire another public relations man, not even one with the connections in the black community that Billy Rowe had. Their position angered me but there was little I could do to persuade them differently. They controlled the funds and in this case *they* stood in the middle of the circle making a decision that displeased me but one over which I had no power this time. We never hired Rowe and that may have been a mistake.

The days began to drag as April ended and spring burst into New York with full force. In this season of the year the senses take on new capabilities, feeling the warmth of the sun, seeing the colorful flowers, assured once more, that the harshness of winter has vanished. It was a bad sign that the freshness of May didn't bring with it a lift to my sagging spirits. Only once in the days after the meeting with Rowe had I felt at all uplifted.

A letter had arrived from Congressman Ronald Dellums, with a paragraph that drove the adrenaline through my system. The letter read, in part:

> "It (the flag) is a symbol of our struggle
> which I am pleased to display. I consider your
> efforts to provide a national symbol, with which
> all Black Americans can identify both commendable
> and necessary to our movement towards solidarity."

He wished me success in the venture and asked that we keep him informed of activities related to the flag.

That letter was shown proudly to the men and to Mabel. Each thought it was indeed a good sign of things yet to come. But there was no movement, no planning going on, nothing to peg as the days flowed one after the other. A lethargy seized all of us, a feeling of wanting to do something but not knowing just what.

Out of the blue, just as despair began to creep across my desk, there was a call from Joe Franklin. He wanted us, Davis and me, to come back and do a radio show with him on May 10th. He had been pleased with the television show and the mail received and he wanted a reprise. It was easy to agree instantly that we would make the show. That was a very good moment, one that excited the group and picked up the pace of conversations over coffee and lunch for the next several days. Davis was on the road and it was difficult to reach him to tell him of the commitment but that too fell into place. He made arrangements to change his schedule so he could be there.

We arrived at the studio feeling more relaxed this time than for any of the other shows. It helped to know that this was radio and there wouldn't be lights and crews to distract me.

Franklin surprised us. He had invited another black man, an historian, to sit in on the show with us. And this man was one of the more acerbic of the black academic community, one whose point of view centered on a steady diatribe against all "white" perspectives of the black man's history. It was more important to him to attack and destroy the writers of America's social history than it was to take the position Davis and I held -- that no matter what had been written the black man in America had earned the right to honor and self respect.

Davis and the man went into it hot and heavy. Franklin was pleased as their discussion of black history burgeoned. I was pleased that Davis gradually assumed command of the discussion coolly correcting statements that were made, statements that drew attention away from the undeniable contributions that black people had made to America's history. In the final analysis he was reminding the man that he was spending energy talking about past injustices recorded in history and none on moving to build a new social history, one in which pride in accomplishment overrode anyone's efforts to circumscribe or denigrate what had already been accomplished. At a point when Dr. Davis was nailing down a comment about black pride in self, Franklin interrupted to say, "That's what the flag is supposed to be about, isn't it?" The question led into my presentation and for the next several minutes the words flowed more smoothly than ever before in my life. In two minutes time I reviewed the meaning of the flag in the most powerful way it had ever been done and then as questions popped about its history, the answers were immediate and complete. For once I had done justice to an interview.

After the show was over, Davis and I stood outside the studio, congratulating each other on what we felt had been the best presentation yet.

Davis said that he saw more self-confidence in me, a sign of growth from the experiences of the last month. I agreed with him, acknowledging that it had not been easy to get accustomed to a world where words were everything and your ability to handle them the measure of you as a person.

He made two suggestions for future courses of action before we parted. He thought that we ought to reconstruct the brochure that accompanied mailings of the flag. Too many important events in the history of the flag had occurred and should be incorporated. And, he asked whether contact had been made with Dr. Benjamin Mays, the venerable President-Emeritus of Morehouse College in Atlanta, Georgia. Both suggestions were appealing; we would pull together photographs and he would rewrite parts of the old brochure while I would make contact with Dr. Mays.

In the days following the radio show there was a run of invitations to speak in the New York City area. The African Students Union at New York University invited me in and other requests came from other campuses. All the appointments were kept as I marvelled that the wheel had turned full round. Once again it was the word-of-mouth process at work. An offer came unexpectedly from a bank in Long Island, wanting to explore the possibility of offering the flag in some form as a premium to customers. An appointment was made to talk with the president of the bank but just before the scheduled meeting a call came asking that I not keep the appointment, that he would be in touch later. He never called back. It was a strange encounter that was never explained. It was the kind of experience that always left me wondering whether the flag was too loaded a concept for *anybody* anywhere to handle. It was like calling Percy Sutton's office to try for an appointment and finding that he was too busy, right now.

In July I went to the Black Expo, held that year in Pittsburgh. The purpose for going, as usual, was to seek out a sizable gathering of black people who might want to absorb word of the flag. The high point of the Expo for me though, was not in making contact with influential black people. The great experience was seeing again the Ozanam Strings, hearing them play and renewing our friendships. The children were bubbling still about the trip to New York; Pitts was full of reminiscences about the experiences. They still wore the emblems on their jackets and asked whether they could order a supply of decals, flags, pins and emblems. They were making presentations of the flag at their performances and wanted to sell the decals and emblems as fund-raisers for trips that were being organized as their fame spread throughout Pennsylvania. It was easy to guarantee them whatever they needed; just hearing their enthusiasm about the flag merited any assistance that could be given in getting them a supply of everything as soon as possible. Promptly upon my return to New York, they were shipped a large consignment of every item we had on hand and just as promptly they disposed of the order and asked for more. The flag was moving out in Pittsburgh!

Davis had made progress with his re-write of the brochure and after the photographs were selected it was a red-letter day when the new brochure went to the printer.

It carried on the front cover a statement that summarized our collective thoughts about what the flag represented even when it seemed that this brochure was going to be the last significant effort to advertise its existence. That statement read, in part:

> A symbol of the pride of Black people
> born out of the sweat of toil, the blood
> of sacrifices and the tears of compassion.

The flag was that and more, so much more that could never be compressed into a single brochure. There was something about the words Davis chose that were important to me though it was hard to describe it even after all the years of trying to make people aware of the flag. I thought about sweat, blood, tears - the fluids of human life, fluids that had washed black people from shore to shore, drowning them in deprivation and despair along the way. Toil and sacrifices had resulted in little space in which to find prosperity, peace or pride, and yet black people had reached into the gifts of their heritage and produced significant achievements that were largely unrecognized even by themselves. We listed some of those accomplishments in this brochure hoping that, once again, the printed word would reach out to whoever read it and remind them that there were achievements to be treasured and honored, achievements that marked the breadth, depth and width of what black people could do given the chance.

We were pleased with the brochure and with the summary of the efforts that it represented for black people in general and the flag's history in particular. Once the brochure was ready for the printer, our attention turned to following up Davis' second suggestion.

A letter had been sent to Dr. Mays and there had been no response. Davis suggested a telephone call and he was right. Dr. Mays' soft voice was kind and encouraging. He had received the letter and was interested in meeting but it would have to be deferred to late in August.

Mabel suggested that if a trip to Atlanta materialized, an effort should be made to contact the Martin Luther King Junior Center for Social Change. There was nothing to be lost from talking with someone there. Following up on that idea, I called the director of the center to ask whether he would give me a few minutes. He sounded enthusiastic about it.

Deciding to take full advantage of being in that city, a letter went to Martin Luther King, Senior requesting an appointment. There was no response within a few days so a call was placed to him, too. He noted that he had gotten my letter and would see me. My calendar was filling up for the impending trip south. Surely something good would come out of one of these appointments at least. Joe and the others were enthusiastic about this trip, recognizing the weight behind the names of the people from whom there were commitments for a few minutes of their time. They sensed the importance of making a connection with someone somewhere, who could open a door just a little crack, enough to shed some light on the flag. The people I was scheduled to see were at the top of a list of influential blacks and that they had granted some time to me was significant!

Chapter 15

The flight to Atlanta was pleasant - a time to relax and enjoy the prospects which lay before me. Almost as soon as I checked into the hotel I turned around and got a cab to the King Center. The director was waiting, affable and impressed by the history of the flag as it was laid out to him.

The Center, at that time, was housed in a building that was its temporary quarters. The office abounded with artists' sketches of the architectural design of the soon-to-be-built permanent Center, an edifice that was to do justice to the memory of Martin Luther King, Jr. For now, the office where we sat was cluttered, full of papers and books and little resembling the resting place for the accumulated memorabilia of one of the most important personalities of the twentieth century.

The director's interest in the flag was evident. He was full of questions about the people to whom the flag had been presented, the responses received from major black organizations, the conferences and meetings that we had attended. We talked intensely for an hour, then he suggested a walk to the nearby campuses to meet some history professors. As we walked along looking at the historic buildings of Morehouse and Spelman College grounds, he remarked that if he were still director of the Center when construction was completed he hoped that the flag would be put on display there with documents that supported it. He thought it would make a worthy addition to the materials that were to be gathered for students of black history to make use of in the future. That was a great offer and it was easy to promise to send whatever he wanted whenever the Center was ready to receive it.

Our stroll took us to several offices on each campus. Introductions were made and the director gave the opening wedge to let me drive home the history of the flag. They were cordial meetings with men who were scholars in black history, men who could sense perhaps more than others the social impact a flag could have for a race of people. Their supportive comments were encouraging. The trip to Atlanta had already paid off and I hadn't yet seen the two men who had drawn me there.

When we returned to his office, the director asked where I was going next, who was yet to be seen. I told him - first, Martin Luther King, Sr.

"You are?" His voice sounded surprised and my guess that he was genuinely caught off guard deepened into surety when he continued, "Do you have an appointment?"

"Yes. I called and talked with him and he invited me to come by for a few minutes."

"Have you ever met him before?"

"No. This is a first time for me and it will be the first time seeing Dr. Mays, too."

"You've got an appointment with him?"

"Yes. And I'd like to see Mrs. King if that could be arranged. Can you get an appointment for me?"

He laughed, a deep, cynical laugh as I sat there wondering what was so funny. He finally choked it off and told me that he couldn't get in to see her himself and that to get an appointment her New York advisors who handled her calendar should have been contacted.

I sat back, looking at him, wondering if the man was off his rocker a little. His demeanor changed, a sober expression settling onto his face as he said that he was the fifth director of the Center in the last few months and that he knew he wouldn't be there long. If he tried to make a move toward getting an appointment for me or anyone else he would be fired on the spot.

I was appalled. Was it true or was it some back-stabbing remark meant to discredit Coretta King because he had probably secured another job and was ready to leave? I felt woefully undereducated about the doings at the Center and knew that perhaps there was no way to broaden that education except to hear it from the inside. Perhaps the man was right after all. If he was, then he had taken considerable risk to accept my telephone calls, to walk with me to the campuses nearby, to sit with me in the office and discuss as freely as he had the state of affairs among the people who had control of the place. It had to take guts to spend time with me if it could have that devastating an effect on him afterwards. I wished him luck and thanked him for his time. He smiled as he shook my hand and told me to call back after Labor Day. He was interested in finding out how my interviews with Reverend King and Dr. Mays would go. He hoped that he would still be there after the holiday. If not - good luck! He thought I would need it.

That marked a peculiar turn to what had begun with so much promise. I was hard pressed to explain the comments the man had made until my meeting with Reverend King.

I arrived at Ebenezer Baptist Church shortly before the scheduled appointment time. Reverend King was not there. I asked if it was all right to wait for a while as it was important to me to see him. I was told it was okay to wait in the church.

There was a phone booth down the street and I went to it, keeping one eye on the walkway to the church in case the Reverend King appeared while I was trying to reach Dr. Mays. He was not at home. The lady who answered suggested that a call be made later. She was sure he would be home soon or that she would hear from him within an hour's time.

I walked back to the church and took a seat in the lobby where it was cool -- and I waited and waited. King hadn't shown yet. After an hour I tried to phone Dr. Mays again. The same gentle voice told me that he had called home and confirmed our appointment but needed to change it to the next day, at 12:15 sharp. He would have only a little time before he was due at another appointment but would see me then. That was a big step and as I returned to the bench inside the church lobby it felt good that that was in place.

The afternoon wore on, the sun beginning to retract its inexorable heat. All hope of seeing Reverend King was just about to slip away when suddenly he walked into the lobby. He had forgotten the appointment and it was not until he had gone into the church office that the secretary told him somebody was waiting in the lobby to see him.

I stood in his presence, introduced myself and told him I was honored to meet him.

"What do you want?"

Plain words, spoken slowly, driving cold nails into my spirit as they were spoken.

I told him that I had come down to show him the Black American Heritage Flag and to talk with him about it, the same flag mentioned in our telephone conversation a few days earlier.

"I remember you now, boy. You the one called about the flag. That's right."

He pushed his eyeglasses up on his face and walked up close to me. I thought he wanted to look into my soul or something. He reached up and moved my tie, telling me in his slow drawl that it was twisted to the side and when you have a big neck you had to keep setting that tie in place. My mouth must have dropped open at this because he chuckled and asked me to sit down. He had certainly caught me off-guard. Sitting down was a relief. My legs had turned rubbery suddenly as I wondered how it was going to be possible to get him to talk about the flag.

He still had control of the conversation. He asked what the flag was about. I began to tell him how I had been going from place to place, seeking assistance in promoting it, looking for cooperation, needing someone who could advise.

His voice cut me off in mid-sentence. He was saying, "You look like a nice boy with spirit and time." His heavy, old man's southern drawl dragged the words out of the side of his mouth and I was dumbfounded, wondering where this was going. Before a word could be uttered, another voice sliced across my thoughts. A woman was calling out...

"Reverend, your yams and greens is done!"

Reverend King stood slowly, hitching up his pants as he rose. The drawling voice continued, "I ain't had nothing to eat and it's going on 3 o'clock in the afternoon. When sister (somebody) cooks greens and yams, it ain't nothing to let go cold. I got to eat that. Can't miss my meal. I wish you luck."

He was gone down the corridor and around the corner so fast it was hard to believe that he had ever been standing in front of me. The interview was over. He didn't offer and yams or greens, much less any assistance or cooperation with the flag.

It was an answer to the questions that had been raised in my mind back at the Center. If this was how things were done in interviews and meetings it was easy to understand why the Center had had five directors in as many months.

I looked in the direction he had gone around the side of the church and

and started out the door. But then I felt impelled to turn around and go into the church itself. At least it was a chance to see the pulpit where Martin Luther King had stood and that would be part of my storehouse of memories of this visit. The door was not locked; the church was empty.

I stood in the vestibule peering through the glass in the inner doors and let my eyes take in the width of the small sanctuary, the choir-stand up front, the massive chairs lining the pulpit, the organ and piano at rest on the sides. I could almost hear the voice of King raised with the fire of his dreams into the rhythms and cant that were so familiar still. It was easy to imagine him standing there, hands gripping the sides of the rostrum, head thrown back as he awakened the audience to the imperatives of being black in America. My mind conjured up a vision of him giving that last sermon, the one where he said he wanted to be remembered as a drum major for justice. Echoes of that voice picked up the words spoken that day - "I tried to help somebody."

I stood there and thought about a man who had tried to help somebody, help me, help my neighbors, help little black children populating a country where their private dreams were the only thing of substance they could depend on. I had come asking today for help and been given second place to a helping of collard greens and yams.

Shaking my head I turned away. It was a short walk to the corner and a cab passing by, right on time.

At my hotel after dinner I lay down with the Atlanta newspaper, trying to read my way out of the despair that was edging in on me. Everything seemed so hopeless. Still - there was tomorrow and the meeting with Dr. Mays. Surely Atlanta would not be a complete bust.

The next morning I packed my bags, got some breakfast and then went looking for a cab to get to Dr. Mays' house. By chance, the same driver who had brought me from Ebenezer Baptist to the hotel, stopped at the curb. We settled on his driving me to the Mays' home and returning to get me to the airport in time for the 1:30 flight back to New York.

When we reached the address, I was impressed with the ranch-style home located on the side of a gentle hill, tall trees whispering above it. A demure lady opened the door, let me put my luggage in the front hall then invited me to sit in the office-library to wait for Dr. Mays. He came around the door in a few minutes, a lean, wiry man whose years were worn gracefully. His voice was slow but strong as he walked up and said his name was Mays. Was I Mr. Charles? We shook hands and sat down. He looked at me and smiled and asked what he could do for me.

I was painfully aware that there were only twenty minutes to compress the history of the flag and make an appeal to him for assistance in any way he could give it. The best approach was the direct one. Mention was made of Alton Davis' name and he nodded in recognition, listening closely as the purpose of the flag was explained.

He murmured that he'd heard something about it but didn't know enough. "Tell me more about it."

His direct look and apparent ease at listening were encouraging and it was easy to launch into the whole of the flag's history, spending only seconds on each of the highlights from the first day to the New York campaign. It was much past my allotted time when the recitation was finished; his questions had provided the opportunity to add bits and pieces of information that completed the picture for him. At the end a flag was laid in front of him and I told him that it was his. He fingered the material, looked at the design. As he held the flag, I thanked him for his time. He looked up, holding my eyes with his.

"Don't thank me for my time. I'm proud of you. Most people come asking for something from me. You have come to give me something. That's important."

He paused only a moment then continued, saying the words that I had wanted so long for someone to say.

"There's nothing wrong with this flag, young man. Black people have had an anthem they call their own for a long time. Why not a flag to go with it?"

As he spoke, a healing warmth permeated my whole body. At last someone had volunteered a statement that made all the years of effort worthwhile.

Dr. Mays was still speaking as a surge of inner peace flooded through me.

"Mr. Charles, you're young. You have time to see the flag become a success. Age is against me. You have to do the one thing I can't do - take time to make this work. Don't stop. You have something of value here and I'm proud of it!"

He stood up, reaching for my hand, still holding the flag in the other hand. I turned and saw that the cab was parked in the driveway outside the office and realized that time had flown and it would be a rush to catch the plane. I had kept Dr. Mays long after the time he had said he could give and he would be late for his next appointment. I was reluctant to leave though.

Somehow the man had given me more encouragement than anyone with whom I had spoken outside the members of the group back in New York. His voice carried assurance in it that the flag was important, that its success would come in time. It was difficult to leave the warmth of that assurance.

He walked with me to the door, asking whether the Schomburg Museum had been approached to display the flag. He urged me to contact Jean Houston again and to use his name as entree to see her. He was certain that an exhibit could be arranged and felt that it would be an appropriate step to take.

As I picked up a piece of luggage, Mays bent down and took the other. He had the heavier piece and it upset me that he would not hand it over. He walked out to the cab with it, turned it over to the cabbie and shook hands again.

"Best of luck, young man. Thank you for coming to see me."

"Thank you, Dr. Mays. The people back in Linden would never believe that Dr. Benjamin Mays carried a piece of my luggage."

He shrugged and smiled. "Don't mean anything, son. Maybe the folks in Linden are luckier than they realize."

I thanked him again and got into the cab. He waved and turned to go into his home.

The cab driver got as far as the corner and his curiosity overtook him. He stopped the car, turned in his seat and asked, "Who you, buddy? You must be somebody important for Dr. Mays to carry your luggage."

"I'm not important, man. He is. He's so much above the rest of us that he can stoop down and still stand taller than we can."

Monday morning I was back at the office, telling over and over the experiences Atlanta had provided. Mabel was pleased that Dr. Mays had been receptive and she urged immediate action on contacting the Schomburg, promising to nag me everyday until that was in place. I smiled. Mabel was a gentle nag, prodding me, urging me to find the extra energy to make the next step. She couldn't have known how deep the exhaustion was running in my body, I was tired. Even the note from WOR, Joc Franklin's station, didn't do much to revive me. The station was extending an invitation to return for still another broadcast. The letter had arrived in my absence. Response to the show Davis and I had done was running strong and they were definitely interested in doing another.

The Labor Day weekend arrived in good time to give me a respite.

My tiredness now dragged at me so openly that my wife asked one night over that weekend, "How much longer can you keep this pace?"

"I don't know. I honestly don't know."

"Are you moving forward any, or going backwards, or marking time? What's happening?"

I shrugged, wondering myself what was happening. "At this point I don't know. I'm fishing still, hoping to catch something that will break this thing wide open. That's what I'm doing."

"You've got to make a life for yourself. This can't continue."

"I know it. I recognize that." I didn't want to admit that she was right. We had bargained for a year's time, a year to invest without question or remonstration. She had given it and more. She was entitled to know how much longer, how many more doors would have to slam shut before it, this quest, was given up. She knew that I was not happy, that failure to make the flag go had worn through my senses of purpose and mission, that I was looking at failure and refusing to admit it was standing right in front of me.

"You have a family and this is affecting them, too."

She was right again. My daily hours in New York had been long and grew even longer when the campaign was at its crest. While the summer days had provided some relief, the work days were still lengthy and my time at home given second place in my list of priorities.

As we talked the words formed in my throat that I didn't want to speak. Finally they tumbled out. I needed to rest, take a break, refuel somehow. All the reserves of energy had been depleted and she was forcing me to acknowledge it openly. When I felt tears gathering in my eyes I knew it was time to let the flag go. It was time to say the course had been run, the race was over and I was vanquished.

That's a terrible admission for a man to make to himself. It strips him of self-esteem, flays the flesh from his sense of manhood to admit that something he tried his heart out to accomplish had not succeeded. It was small consolation that there were thousands of people who were, by now, fully aware of the flag and what it was intended to represent. There were millions more who didn't and I had no way to reach them. Dr. Mays had said I had time to make the flag go. But I was too tired. It seemed no use. I had to give up.

There was left only the task of preparing the display for the Schomburg Museum, sifting through pictures and articles and sorting them down to the few that might tell the saga of the flag succinctly and positively.

A picture of Nancy Wilson accepting the flag at the Apollo was placed among those for display. There were some children in the background and the picture embodied somehow the essence of the campaign - the children who had made it a success for themselves and the talents that both she and they used to give expression to the capabilities of black people. There was a picture of a presentation made by Gleason and myself in the early days of the flag and it was included to remind the viewer of the small beginnings of it all. The flag that had flown over Newark City Hall was to be the center-piece. It had been wrapped and packed away all these years, waiting for the right place to be shown publicly and this was it. Some news articles describing the earliest word of the flag's existence would explain what the flag was about. A couple of copies of the new brochure made the bottom line for the exhibit.

Jean Houston had been cordial in our discussions focused on arranging the display. She thought it was appropriate and looked forward to the day in mid-September that we had settled on for delivery of the cabinet to the museum. It was planned that I would bring the items for the exhibit on the next day and that I would arrange it myself. The business of the Museum would not be interrupted to take care of that task.

The flag would be given a final resting place and I would see to it alone.

Chapter 16

The subway car was nearly empty. An old woman sat across from me, handbag clutched tightly to her chest, her head against the window, eyes closed. That was a brave thing to do on a subway in New York City. She must have been very tired.

A group of teenagers sat up front in the car, laughing and joking about something that had happened to a friend earlier in the day. They looked old enough to have summer jobs, but jobs were scarce for black teenagers in the city and across the nation in 1972.

As we neared 135th Street, the steady rhythm of the wheels slowed; metal creaked and screeched as the train began entry to the station.

The teenagers got up abruptly, the group already intent on the next event in their lives, waiting for them up on the hot pavement of Harlem. The old woman shifted in her seat, peered out the window to confirm where she was and settled back to ride it out a while longer,

I took the box from the seat beside me and headed out the car, up the stairs and into the sunlight above. The box was not heavy. It held the mint flag, photographs, and the news clippings and a few small white cards. It fit easily under my arm as I walked the streets on my way to the Schomburg Museum.

The building was not very imposing in appearance, belying the wealth of black history that it sheltered. I stopped for a moment outside the entrance and looked along the sidewalk at the people moving in and out of storefronts, standing in little clusters here and there, children running and screaming at each other. This was Harlem, all right. Hot sun steaming the dingy buildings, cars double-parked, gutters overflowing with debris, home-made signs announcing the wares in the stores, people marking time, making time, wasting time.

I went inside the Schomburg, talked for a few minutes with the receptionist, told her I'd be only a short while setting up the exhibit and then I gave her a lapel pin. She smiled softly as she looked at the pin in her hand and then told me to take all the time I needed.

The cabinet was against a far wall in the large room, placed there the day before in readiness for the display. It was a tall cabinet, dark walnut wood, glass front, three shelves. I opened the doors, dusted the shelves and it only took seconds, it seemed, to put the photographs on the top shelf, the brochures and laminated clippings at the bottom, and finally the flag, folded so that the golden wreath was centered, on the middle shelf. The small white cards were last, placed flat on the shelves to identify the faces of the famous who had received flags at one presentation or another, and the slightly larger card that described the flag and its symbols.

When everything was in place I closed the doors and stepped back to satisfy myself that the display was visually pleasing and then walked back to the receptionist's desk.

"You didn't take long after all," she said.

I smiled at her and agreed. There was not much point in telling her how long I had been living the Black American Heritage Flag and today was one more event in its history but one of great significance to me.

I left the Schomburg Museum, walking again through the streets, feeling the day's heat penetrate my summer suit, my mind skimming through the hundreds of things that still had to be done.

The subway platform was empty except for a group of nursery-school children, adults circling and reminding them constantly, "Everybody stay together; everybody hold hands." Their words were a constant stream, flowing out and reverberating in the cavern underground. Their voices rose even higher as the train rushed in, urging more care to hold onto each other until the doors opened. They and I filtered through the exiting passengers to find seats in the steamy car.

The children's voices were excited and full of wonder as the train left the station. "OOOOH, it's dark down here." "Looka there!" "What's that noise?" I listened to their innocence proclaim itself and was pleased that someone would give them this new experience this day.

The day's experience had been one of the most rewarding of my life. The flag had been placed on exhibit in a museum renowned for its collection of black history artifacts. Now the flag was at rest. The wheels of the train settled into their hypnotic cadence, the shifting motion of the car luring my body to relax for the ride. I thought of the people and events that had led to this day.

Gleason. He would be proud today. He would be in sorrow as I was that it marked the end of a dream.

A steady stream of people crossed my consciousness. The mayor and councilmen of Linden who had denied us the right to unfurl the flag, the members of the Crispus Attucks Society who had been the first to say bluntly that the flag was nothing because it didn't have ships and planes and guns behind it. People praising the Lord in a cellar church and accepting the existence of the flag with pride. Organizers of the Poor People's March wanting more money then we had to give. Neighbors and friends wanting a cut of the "action" but refusing to fly the flag in front of their homes. A minister trembling in fear of what would happen if we came in to his church and black students posting the banner in their college rooms. The NAACP and the Urban League people who had talked me into caring about black pride and then refused to deal with the tangible symbol of that pride. Lee Winkler and Joe Zavlik and a group of white men who put money into the effort out of a sense of its importance. And Dave Topf and Clyde and the boys of the Youth Leadership Council who had pulled me through a time of despair and given me something to cherish - the certainty that young black people were determined to become somebody and willing to work to achieve their goals. The children of the Ozanam Strings, talented, disciplined, proud of themselves.

LeRoi Jones and Martin Luther King, Senior. And Dr. Benjamin Mays saying HE was proud of the flag.

The train pulled into my station and it was a short walk to the office and the true beginning of the end.

That night I called Dr. Davis to let him know that the work was completed, the flag was at the Schomburg. I thanked him for all that he had done and told him that I had reached the end of the run. He was silent for a moment then wished me well. He asked that we stay in touch. We would!

The hardest part was to come, telling Joe and Mabel and the others of my decision. They had let me stand for so long in the circle of lonely decision-making, waiting to hear what my opinion was on whatever came up -- except the decisions to fire Bill and to not hire Rowe. This time they were waiting quietly to hear me say out loud what they already suspected. My withdrawal from the project would close down the entire effort. No more emblems would tumble from the machines, no more t-shirts would be silk-screened, no more buttons would flip from the molds. It was truly finished, not just for me but for them too.

I sat with Joe early on the morning of September 10th. We sipped coffee without talking, letting the hot liquid warm us. It was an unusually brisk day for that time of the year and heat wasn't turned on yet in the building. A cup of coffee warmed the hands and the insides even when you didn't need its stimulation. I was already edgy, dreading the chore of finding the words to tell Joe I was pulling out. He was watching me, waiting for what he knew was coming.

"Joe, got to tell you something. I don't know that I can last any longer at this. I feel like a fighter throwing left and right without any sting to it. Nothing's worked out."

"You can't give it up now. There's too much time invested in your dream."

"I know that. Everybody has given so much and I realize they don't have the time or the reason to continue with it. To not close down now is to drag out the burial. The funeral's already been held."

"That's so morbid, Mel. You are tired. I've been watching you. Everything seems to be going out from you and nothing coming back. You've had a lot on your mind. Are you sure a few weeks rest and a change of scenery wouldn't do the trick and bring you back ready to try again?"

"No. A few weeks won't do it, Joe. I've got to close it down. Before the month is out my desk will be clear."

"Well, you can't just leave like that. Everybody will have to know. We'll have to have a meeting."

"I'll leave that to you."

"Oh no. You call the meeting. You arrange it for when you want it and everybody will be here in your schedule. They will have questions and only you can answer them, so you arrange it."

I contacted them all. Mabel, Ted, Vic, Morty. They would come, struggling to find the words to convince me that some rest and relaxation would make the difference, knowing deep inside themselves that mine was not just a tiredness of the body. My spirit had been wounded from too many rebuffs, too many times knocking on doors that would not open, too many times explaining to people what the flag meant to me and finding them responding with a kind of "How nice" attitude. The major black organizations had shown no interest, individuals of importance had chosen to eat literal and figurative yams and collard greens instead of chewing on the merits of the flag and finding a way to make it palatable to the millions of black Americans I wanted to reach. Help had come, yes, from a group of white men who had a vested interest in the success of the flag but who, after all, would not have gone as far as they did if there had not been a genuine belief in the rightness of the whole concept. And here they were, trying to find words to dissuade me from closing down the project.

I was determined. There is an old saying about throwing good money after bad. Their good money had supported the effort for more than a year. We had made mistakes in judgment and omissions in action - it was true. But they had stood beside and behind me through the months of trying to make things a success. There were no words to describe how I felt about their attempts to help and it was difficult to keep control of my emotions. They knew that and tried small talk about how good the exhibit looked at the Schomburg, telling me indirectly that they had made the trip to Harlem to see it for themselves. Finally Ted, the usually silent one, opened the floodgates for my decision to flow through. He spoke quietly as though he didn't want to disturb the reverie that overwhelmed me, sitting in the room where so many decisions had been made over those many months.

"You know, Mel, you have to be a special sort of person. You've faced more rejections than I could take and you got up off the canvas each time. Can't you give it one more try?"

"No, I can't. And you already know what I want to say."

"Yes, I do. We do and we understand what you're saying and why you're saying it. We just wanted you to know that we will support you in whatever decision you make."

I looked around the room, taking measure once more of a remarkable group of people: Morty, another of the more silent of the group but always there; Vic, ebullient Vic, ready with a joke and his cash when the need arose; Ted, the most silent of them all, watching everything and everybody, scrupulous in his sense of detail when it came to preparing the wares that carried the flag; Joe, the sensitive one who had tried hard to find the right person to steer the project through to a successful climax. Joe had shared office space with me, making room in his private empire for an outsider, offering the nearness of his presence when I needed to spill out a day's happenings. I would miss him a great deal. I had come to know him perhaps best of all the men and respected him for his sense of balance and perspective even in the worst of moments.

Mabel sat still, absorbing the weight of the feelings that were overwhelming me. Her sensitivity and strength had been incomparable. She had been every bit as necessary for my emotional survival through the disappointments encountered in the project as she had been vital in making suggestions aimed at helping us make progress in reaching out to people. Davis was not there, but his place in the group was felt. He had been the intellectual, assessing coolly the steps we took, offering a perspective that carried with it a sure knowledge of the historical worth of any move. He had been a very special element in the group, presenting to the manufacturers a quality of thought they had not likely encountered before in all their business dealings. He would tell me later that he felt the businessmen could have offered more financial support to keep the project viable yet he realized that without my wholehearted wish to continue there was nothing they could do or say.

Mabel took my hand as the meeting ended. She was soon to move to Chicago and would be busy clearing out her office in Manhattan. She wished me well and asked me to stay in touch. With a quick hug she was gone.

The words had been said; the last meeting over. I shook hands around, thanked each one.

In the last week of September I cleared a few things from my desk each day. On Friday morning there was only a little left to dispose of and I knew that it wouldn't take long to do that. I drove into the city late that day, pulling into the parking garage near the office and finding that it was nearly full. The attendant, a wiry old man named Willie, was sitting just inside the door, surprised to see me arrive so much later than usual.

He came around to the driver's side of my car, opening the door with his usual "Good morning, Mr. Charles."

He asked how I was feeling. I told him, "Fine, Willie, just fine."

He motioned toward my car. "If I had your money I'd throw mine away." It was a pointless little statement he often made, a way to engage someone in conversation for a few minutes to break the day's monotony of parking and retrieving cars. I had usually laughed at the little joke, Knowing that Willie probably stashed every tip he made and had a healthy nest egg put away somewhere for his retirement to his home town down south. So this time I didn't laugh. I told him "If I had my money in your bag, you couldn't do nothing, Willie. You couldn't even go to South Carolina walking."

Willie turned serious.

"I want to go to South Carolina, Mr. Charles. People here fight, kill each other. It's not safe here and I'm getting old. I want to be where people show a little respect for each other and some kindness to us senior citizens."

"Yes, Willie, it would be nice if people showed some respect for each other." By then I was out of the car and turning to head for the office. I looked back at Willie and realized that I would not be coming here again and would not trade stories any more.

"Willie, this is my last day here. I just wanted you to know I won't be coming back."

"But what about the flag, Mr. Charles? What's going to happen to the flag?"

"It's going to be retired, Willie. Just like you're going to retire soon."

"I know what you mean. You work hard and don't see any results for your labors. That's why I'm gon' retire and move back to South Carolina, leave this rat-infested city and get a little piece of land and put me up a brick house. Bricks don't cost much down home. I'm going to live in some peace for the rest of my days."

"That's great, Willie. Tell you what; when I get the chance to drive down 95, I'll stop by to see you and we'll eat some of that sweet corn you've talked about."

"Ok, Mr. Charles. That sure would be nice."

We laughed and shook hands. Willie didn't really think I was serious.

Upstairs the place was gloomy. Joe was there, keeping to his office. Ted came in about 10 o'clock, staying for only a moment and then leaving. The secretary was busy at her typewriter, employees were working the machines in the back. The place had its usual hum of activity but somehow it was different that morning.

I opened the desk drawers, searching them to be sure that they had been cleaned out completely. I didn't take time off for lunch, wanting to finish as soon as possible. The few things left in the drawers and file were put into the cardboard box I had gotten from the production area. About 2:30, I was closing the last drawer when suddenly I noticed Joe standing in the doorway watching me. I don't know how long he had been there. When he caught my eye, he said he had to go out for a while. He left.

Not long after that, the secretary called through the door as she pulled on her light coat. "Mr. Charles, I'm leaving. Do you want me to make sure the janitor closes up?"

"Yes, And thanks. I won't be long."

My desk top was clear now. Everything of value had been put in the box. Most of the employees had gone; the machines had closed for the day. The janitor was somewhere out in the back, assuring himself that the doors were locked tightly.

My back was to the window as I sat at the desk. Sunlight streamed over my shoulder onto the surface of the desk, catching little specks of dust and making them appear like miniature jewels tossed carelessly on the wooden top. As I sat there for longer than I know, the sun dropped lower until it highlighted the black telephone on the edge of the desk. I reached over and unplugged it knowing that the last call had been made to the office of the Black American Heritage Flag. The line would be cut off, put out of service just as I felt I was cutting myself off from a vital connection.

The stillness in the office was suddenly overpowering. There had always been so much action, bustle, movement going on and it had been energizing to be part of that space and that time when things were snapping and jumping in anticipation of the successful promotion of the flag.

I put my hands flat on the desk and shoved myself up from the chair. Everything was packed. There was no point in staying any longer.

While I waited for the elevator I looked around once more at the familiar corners and corridors that had greeted me for so long. I hoped that somehow I had left a mark on the place, a sign that I had been there for a while, trying to accomplish a task that had been set a long time ago over a cup of tea in a friend's living room.

The elevator doors closed and the loft was gone from sight.

Willie was still at the garage when I turned the corner. He jumped up, saying, "I just saw Mr. Joe. He said you were leaving. I thought you were joking. You're not really going, are you?"

"Yes, Willie, I am. No joke. I'm taking an early retirement with the flag. Going to put it out to pasture for now."

"Hey, Mr. Charles, you a real good man. Don't give it up."

"I'm not really giving it up, Willie. I just got to rest for a while. You can't ever give up something that's a part of your breathing and living, but you do have to let some things rest now and then."

I handed him a tip and got into my car. He stood there, turning the coins over in his hand. He was every man for a moment, some symbolic black every man, ageless yet ancient, worn but strong, tired of the endless rat race that he couldn't seem to win, rejuvenated by the thought that there was a better place and willing to make the changes that were necessary to get to that place. Willie seemed to metamorphose in front of my eyes. I could see the eyes of my childhood friend Willie peer at me through those of the garage attendant. That Willie had lost his race with life's dangers. There was no flag he could salute. He and the boys of Frog's Hollow had been swallowed up in the miasma of the ghetto that had been home for us. I had gotten out and tried to do something worthwhile. I hoped that they could somehow know that my efforts had been for them and for all the black children who had to began their lives in the shadow of an oil storage tank, playing out the fantasies of success in the gutters and littered fields of their streets. The Willie of my childhood faded from view as a voice cut through the memories.

"Don't forget, Mr. Charles. If you ever come to South Carolina look up old Willie."

"I will, I'll look you up, pal. It's been good to know you."

I pulled out of the garage and drove slowly to the corner where the traffic light was red. While I waited for it to turn, my eyes strayed to two young black boys pushing their bicycles across. One bike had a flat tire so they were both walking home. As they reached the sidewalk totally unaware of me, I saw that they each had an emblem on the back of their jackets.

Black is Beautiful.

Black American Heritage Flag..

Epilogue

There are several boxes in the basement of my parents' home, stacked in a corner and gathering dust. The boxes contain the memorabilia of the six years that were the active life of the Black American Heritage Flag. In those boxes are the letters, news clippings, brochures, t-shirts, decals emblems, buttons and lapel pins that were packed away that day in September 1972. Somewhere among the collection of things there are several flags, some small and a few of the largest ones that were produced. The collapsible pole that Gleason and I used is at the bottom of a box. The design flag that hung for years in the basement of my home is wrapped in plastic, packed last of all the things that are the visible signs of the flag's existence.

It has been years since that September when the project unfolded. In those years my life has changed again and again.

I have dealt with the overpowering sense of failure that tore me apart as I left the office on that last day. Even seeing the emblems on the boys' jackets gave me no more than a momentary lift to the intense and deadening feeling that somehow I had failed as a person, as a man, when the only avenue left open was that of closing down the project. That feeling was perhaps the worst of all the experiences that came my way in the years of working for the flag. The sense of being burdened with failure did not lift and leave me until this manuscript was begun. It was only in the recounting of the events that marked the history of the flag that it became clear to me that if you have tried to do something and failed you are infinitely better than if you tried to do nothing and succeeded.

And it has helped too, to know that the flag was not a failure. It touched the lives and minds and hearts of many thousands of Black Americans, how many I can never really know.

I have changed, grown, found some personal peace in the knowledge that I have tried to bring the flag to as many black people as I could.

I have found no peace in the knowledge that the motives and thoughts that led to the creation and design of the flag still have merit. Things have not changed much for black people. Conditions of life today give little space in which to find prosperity, peace or pride. A narrow corridor marks the direction and the horizon toward which we move. We are confined; we are driven like cattle to begin our lives for the most part, in poverty and to die the same way. We watch our children grow into adulthood without a sure sense that they really can be whatever they want to be. They dance and sing, do their lessons in school, but they do not yet grow up to occupy seats of power or manage major corporations or hold executive positions that bring the weight of their intellectual potential to bear on the lives of most Americans. Those few who make it through the barriers that history imposes (despite legislation and the "law of the land"), sometimes appear to forget the shape and form of the tree from which they have come, a tree whose roots lie deep in a history of ancestral greatness, whose branches have borne the fruit of individual accomplishments, and whose trunk is scarred with the deep cuts that slavery and degradation and poverty and misery drove into the great natural strength that characterized the tree.

We sometimes forget our common heritage, separating ourselves one from the other by the social lines we have drawn across the face of that heritage, lines that mark us off into groups by the shades of our skin color or the texture of our hair, by degrees earned and positions held, by the size and contents of our cars and houses. We are torn apart by the wedges driven between us, wedges that make us suspicious of each other and our motives, wedges of fear that we must still bend to the will of some "Massa" who holds sway over our thoughts and our actions. Yet, when you scratch below the surface of our differences, there is a consuming unanimity that speaks of our blackness. You can see it in the responses to our music, responses that tell everyone that the sounds have soaked beneath the skin, creating that subtle shift of shoulder and hips, moving out from the soul. You can feel it in the voices of those who remind us that we are brothers still and that our survival depends on accepting the burden of helping one another since nobody else will. You can tell it when college students prepare themselves seriously for the new technology and the challenge of work with machines and minds far different from any that their parents experienced. You know it when the lines form for a paltry handful of jobs and the black men and women waiting for an application tell you they want to work, want to earn their way, to be productive and able to care for their families without assistance.

We are still and shall always be, black people who can rejoice in the achievements of forebears long dead and the ever-growing list of attainments made each day by some individual among us. We can rejoice in our literature that sings and soars with the spirit of an indomitable people who may be down but never out of life's game, music that lifts the feet from the muck of our cities to the rainbows that exist in our dreams. We are a people whose greatness is still untold; we wait for each new line to be added, hoping that someone will finally tell it all and that everyone will know that we were and are a people whose heads can be held high with pride.

We all know we are black people no matter how far from the tree of our ancestry we may fall.

We have no tangible symbol of that affirmation except that which resides in the mind and spirit and soul. The flag was offered as a symbol of our ancestral connectedness tempered with the aspirations and hopes we hold as citizens of this country. It might have served us in the same way that other hyphenated Americans find to identify themselves, a rallying point to place at the prow of their gatherings in this land of promise, freedom, justice. WE, black people, stand on the sidewalks and watch our fellow Americans march in their parades, proclaiming through their celebrations their ancestral remembrances. They captivate us as they remind us time and again of the diversity of the American people.

We do not parade with a symbol of our ancestry or heritage. We do march, forced as we are, our feet growing weary with the beat that compels too many of us to the unemployment windows, the welfare offices, the clinics, the food-stamp offices, forming the lines that snake through the souls of our children's futures. We march because we must, because we have not yet found the key to the doors that lock us away from the benefit of being American - the freedom to achieve the greatness that lies within us as individuals and as a people.

Perhaps it is that a flag could not serve as a key to that realization.

Yet I know that despite all that has happened to us since we arrived in this country we have achieved somehow, we have found in the remembered strength of our ancestors and the fruit of our own labors that there is cause to celebrate being black. That we have survived at all is testimony to that strength and greatness and that survival is warrant enough to justify finding pride in who we are.

The flag was meant to symbolize that pride.

It still does..

The Black American Heritage Flag Society, a non-profit organization, recommends use of a 30-minute ceremony for unfurling the flag, with the following elements:

****

Introduction of the flag	-Local Sponsor (organization president)
Music	-School Choral Group
History of the flag	-Councilperson (who introduced the local resolution)
Recognition of citizen	-Honoree:A citizen who exemplifies pride, responsibility, identity, dignity, efforts to improve the community
Flag unfurling	-Chapter president, Mayor, Councilperson, Honor
Reciting of the pledge	-Student Scholar in the community
Music	-Lift Ev'ry Voice and Sing: Audience

****

Red Zuber by Murrell Violet Goodwin

Black American Heritage Flags and memorabilia may be ordered from:

THE BLACK AMERICAN HERITAGE FLAG
P.O. BOX 202
EAST ORANGE, NEW JERSEY 07019
(201) 366-1776

FLAGS: 8" x 10" ....$ 4.00
2' x 3' 25.00
3' x 5' 75.00
3' x 5' (with oak pole and base) 135.00
5' x 8' 140.00

LAPEL PIN: 5.00
T-SHIRT: (sm, med, large, x-large) 15.00
DESK FLAG SET 5.00
BASEBALL CAPS.. 15.00
LICENSE PLATES (B.A.H.F.) 10.00

(All orders F.O.B., East Orange, New Jersey)